As It Were

As It Were

Life at a Slight Angle
to the Universe

Joseph Roccasalvo

To order additional copies of this book, contact:
Xlibris Corporation
1-888-795-4274
www.Xlibris.com
Orders@Xlibris.com
84634

Contents

Posso promettere di non dire nulla che sia falso. Ma non vorrò dire tutto. Riservo a me il diritto di mentire per omissione. A meno che non cambi idea.

I can promise to say nothing untrue, but I shall not want to say all; and I reserve the right to lie by omission. Unless I change my mind.

Giuseppe di Lampedusa

Part I

Passato Remoto

i

I begin this memoir in a state of acute reluctance. I'm not even sure I can call it a memoir, for my story consists of reminiscences extending over seven decades in which the breaks are exceptionally long. My record of events begins with the alpha of infancy, full of boundless affection, and ends with the omega of adulthood when choices have narrowed and aging is the clearest sign of movement. The memories I set down are taken from several periods so detached in time and space that I have to fill in the gaps. I'm happy to do so, for I chanced to come into contact with persons of genius who became my friends. I'm fortunate to have in safekeeping a body of their work that is still unpublished. What they share in common is fidelity to fine writing, and my intent is to ensure them public recognition.

We are told that every seven years not a corpuscle stays the same. If this is physiologically true, how much more the changes in mind and heart. Despite variations, I'm driven to reclaim friendships whose pattern has persisted over fifty years. In remembering them, I'm retrieving my own life as well. Try as I may, I cannot do otherwise, for the events I relate are so lodged in my memory that they refuse to budge. Why do they make a claim on constancy? This memoir seeks an answer although its pursuit is a major challenge. Most of the persons of whom I write use standard forms of communication. Some have a computer and cell phone, others an e-mail address or a BlackBerry. Still others have only a landline but never respond in person. Call them, and a machine invites you to leave a message to which they fitfully reply. Surely, you say, they at least own a typewriter. They do not. The letters they write, though the number is small, are penned in ink. I have learned to respect such idiosyncrasies as a function of friendship and even to support them. Like condiments judiciously used, they spice my prose and enhance the flavor of my story.

In composing this memoir, I cannot say I've invented nothing. Breaks in my contact with friends resemble a desert whose emptiness forfeits any trace of life. So I have appealed to my imagination and filled in the blanks with scenes in which I never took part. Even so, I have sides of the puzzle and clusters of interlocked pieces. In the overall picture holes prevail. The liberties I've taken to create coherence are meant to incite the reader to turn the page. While this account is biographical, it is not an autobiography. I've dispensed with documentary material on which further biographical studies might be based, should my fiction ever attain prominence. Still, this memoir is not composed in haiku where minimalism is prized and less is viewed as more. Sometimes less is simply less. I adhere to the principle that truth resides in the detail. In the casual remark or trivial gesture, an explosion of meaning sometimes occurs by which one unaccountably perceives the whole.

ii

I ask myself the question: how was it possible I became who I am? What were the precedents, parental and familial, that fashioned my outlook on life? How did infantile events affect my personality and vocational choices? Researchers in child psychology calculate that about half the variation in personality is owed to genes while the rest is shaped by environment. How is difficult to say. Yet here I am: a Catholic priest and a weekly homilist; a Buddhist specialist and comparative historian of religions; a fiction writer and an occasional playwright. I live in an apartment whose interior design resembles one of Kyoto's traditional inns. The research I do requires my alternating among a dozen languages, and I'm delighted to be in the company of those who are equally adept. If I had my druthers, I would add to my practice of Japanese calligraphy, a breeding pond for goldfish.

In composing this memoir, I'm tempted to write no name on the dedication page except the words: "To Our Many Selves." This inscription is not meant to glorify psychosis expressed in disparate lives. I'm addressing what I call the maestro personality. Here the ego, like Toscanini, taps the podium and leads the musical instruments in playing together. Tuning up sounds discordant, but oh, what a glorious sound when cacophony yields to the swell of a full orchestra performing in unison.

In seeking an answer to the questions I've raised, I turn to my mother's diaries for 1941 and 1942, which encompass the first two years of my life. Here are her pertinent remarks pieced together in one continuous statement. I have combined entries that begin when I'm three months old.

1941

I decided to send Joseph to my mother-in-law's house to be taken care of. I cannot handle twin babies without help and many times I find myself alone. They were all surprised and glad to have him. Especially thrilled was my father-in-law whose name Joseph shares. I missed him so much that I dressed up Michael and went to see Joseph at the house. I love them equally yet cannot take care of both babies, though I want them both near me. I couldn't stop kissing Joseph. One day has passed and already he looks different. I'm hoping that if I have help, I will take him back. I am annoyed at Pina, my mother-in-law's sister, for showing partiality to Joseph. I made it understood that I want both babies to receive the same affection and treatment. They love Joseph more because he looks like the Roccasalvo side. I don't think it is fair to Michael, who is a beautiful baby. If I see that their affection toward Joseph becomes too pronounced, I shall take him back if only to prove that Michael is not to be neglected. I should like to nurse them both as long as possible.

Joseph seems to prefer my milk to the bottle. What an enchanting baby. Though he is not as good-looking as Michael, he is very appealing and exceptionally attractive. He was so beautiful, sleeping alone in his twins' carriage, that I kissed him quite a lot. As I looked at him, he smiled as if he knew me. When awake, he looks so pretty and is so clever. He coos continually and has such a beautiful smile. My mother-in-law is so crazy about him that she will not part with him even for a few days. But as time passes, Joseph knows me as only one of the crowd around him. He was very playful tonight. He laughed out loud, and I could have eaten him up; he was so cute. Michael and Joseph share an equal affection. I gave Joseph to my mother-in-law only for a few months. I want to take him back, but I feel so tired. It's continued drudgery from morning until night. What a life for me!

When Joseph visits here, it seems strange to have him in my house sharing Michael's crib, high chair, swing, and toys. He fits in nicely in his new surroundings. Michael and Joseph stare at each other and are quite aware of each other's presence. But Michael cries if I hold Joseph in my arms, while Joseph stares at me when I hold Michael. He has, I believe, the feeling that I belong to him. Though he doesn't know yet that I am his mother, he makes a fuss over me when he sees me. Michael clamors for me and will not stay with anyone else. Today I took Joseph for a couple of hours, and he seemed content playing in the pen, high chair, and other places; however, Michael cries when I pick Joseph up and makes an attempt to hit him. Joseph was so quiet and serious. Everyone tells me I ought to keep the twins together. I wish I could. Perhaps I shall take Joseph back on March 1. It will be a year since he left. The other day he was so affectionate. He cuddled close to me as if to say, "Aren't you my mother whom I see every now and then?"

1942

Today I'm going with Pina to get her citizenship papers. I feel more like staying home, but after what she does for Joseph I cannot refuse her. It's been several days since I saw Joseph who now calls me Auntie. Pina and my mother-in-law are quite concerned that he will remain with them for nine more months. Even if it means added work, I know it's best to have the two babies together to develop brotherly love. Days pass when

I haven't seen Joseph and I miss him. When I finally see him, he seems so indifferent to me. After not visiting for a week, he practically forgets me. I would take him back even now if my mother-in-law would give him to me, but she won't.

When Joseph is here, he sometimes becomes irritable and cries quite often. Michael wants to embrace and kiss him, but Joseph pushes him away. Ordinarily, Joseph is very good. He sleeps and eats well and enjoys being in my house. But Michael seems so jealous that he pushes Joseph and hits him, and Joseph cries. When he speaks, he says Italian words like bacalà or English words like coffee pot.

I went to see him when I had heard he was up all night, crying and fretting. My mother-in-law was disgusted. I offered to take Joseph back, but she said no. He is getting wilder by each day, but he is so cute that I could eat him up alive. Michael is always after him to hug and kiss him, but then slaps him down. He gets jealous whenever Joseph comes near me. Joseph still calls me Auntie, and sometimes when he spends the entire day with me, he doesn't eat or sleep. His mind is on Pina or his home around the corner, and he cries when I try to put him to sleep. I go to bed exhausted.

I'm glad the twins are two years old, and I'm hoping they will be well and strong in 1943.

What have I learned from my mother's diaries? At about three months old, I'm given away to be cared for by Grandma Roccasalvo, Pina, and two aunts: Mary and Rose. I'm visited and nursed fitfully by my mother who is anemic, generally exhausted, and given to fainting spells. My brother Michael is colicky and my sister Joan is sick with childhood illnesses like scarlet fever and pneumonia. Temporary departure from my parental home to "the house around the corner" is at first a necessity that later becomes a fixed arrangement. The situation continues for two and a half years during which I learn to speak Sicilian as my first language. I know my mother only as auntie, and I view my brother Michael as a congenial stranger; he is so jealous of any intimacy with our mother whom he calls "my mother" that he pushes me away. I'm not hurt by his rejection because around the corner I'm hugged, kissed, and petted as I pass from one admirer to the next.

The key to my later global awareness lies in infancy. There I was exposed to a diversity that morphed into a piety without borders. Psychology tells us that infantile bonding with the mother or maternal substitute is the source of trust. For me, Mother—that biological matrix which nurtures unconditionally—was more than one person. It was a group composed largely of doting women. From that inner circle, I learned that by presence alone I could please either singly or in numbers. As an infant, I developed multiple patterns of response based on relationships with several caregivers, especially my paternal grandmother and her half sister. In those instances, when I had a weak attachment to my biological mother—since she came and went unpredictably, overreacting when she sees me but then taking leave—the secure connection to my grandmother and great-aunt took on a compensatory role.

"Compensatory" is putting it mildly. Everyone's darling, I was fondled and nuzzled. Those marks on my neck from soft biting were epidermal evidence of an affection that was skewed but always on tap. In fact, my earliest memory is my grandparents' dining room. I see a table laden with dishes while I'm in the middle, propped up in a bassinet. My father's two sisters, when not reaching for food, reach for me. Their faces overhead do more than smile. They beam. They pick me up and hand me to my grandmother's half sister, Pina, my most ardent admirer. As she presses me to her bosom, generous even by Italian standards, she says in Sicilian, "*Kistu beddu picciottu è fiatu mi*" (This beautiful baby is my breath).

The conclusion is clear. As an infant, I was an emotional polytheist; pluralism was my natural element. It's here—and I'm guessing without an analyst's couch—that I learned to accept multiple viewpoints. It confirmed my mother's later assertion: "You have to have latitude and longitude of vision." She said this as she shaped the world roundly with both hands. Her gesture amounted to a cosmopolitanism of the spirit that preferred range to concentration. Sensibility, she insisted, must be directed over the broadest possible sphere. It's global.

I have never married, a state precluded by my religious vocation and sanctioned by my personality. I've been told that I go to the limits of persons quickly, and would feel captive if I were conjugally bound to one individual. (I still lose my breath in a small space, especially when an elevator lingers between floors.) My affective life too has the overreach enjoined by my mother, and is directed broadly over countless friends. I facetiously call them my conglomerate lover, for they represent every race, creed, culture, language, gender, and sexual orientation. Anything less than this motley group would be gagging. Priesthood and temperament conspire agreeably in this match of circumstance.

Still, what remains is the issue of separation anxiety and how I dealt with it. Before I turned six months old, it was not an issue. I showed little special attachment to my grandmother, Pina, or my mother. They came and went without inducing distress, and when left alone, I did without. But at ten months, during protracted visits to my parents, I reacted by crying and fussing, and I called for Pina or my grandmother. At bedtime, it became a struggle when I refused care from all but those two primary caregivers. I recognized Pina and Grandma Roccasalvo as unique individuals. But I lacked the ability to grasp that they still existed when out of sight. Though they lived around the corner, since they could not be seen they were "gone" forever. So I learned to accept inconstancy as constant. Disposed to a Buddhist sensibility, I was internalizing early the first noble truth, *sabbe anicca*: all things are impermanent. The newly acquired relationship with my birth mother caused me distress, and I reacted with prolonged bouts of crying. Only gradually did I grasp I was not being abandoned: that Grandma Roccasalvo and Pina would return; that my mother would be accessible. My anxiety diminished and I flourished under the protection of three different but devoted caregivers. But the impermanence returned with a vengeance when at two and a half I was wrenched from my home around the corner, moving back with my parents, sister, and twin brother.

"Jofis speaks so funny," Michael would say when we rode the train together. Mother would tell me in Italian, *Stai zitto* (Be quiet) so I would not attract attention. It was singularly odd to have identically dressed twins sharing unidentical languages. I had first to learn English and then accept Michael as my brother. Always resourceful, my mother achieved both ends by teaching us dramatic skits. At three years old [sic], Michael and I recited together the Gettysburg Address, sang a medley of radio commercials, and ended with our signature song: "We are the Roccasalvo twins you hear so much about/The people stop and stare at us whenever we go out/We're noted for our speeches and songs and everything we do/ Most everybody likes us/We hope you like us too" until we reached the rousing climax: "We are a team, rah rah/We've got the steam rah rah/ For this is Roccasalvo Day." I was too young to recognize the boasting and to deplore it. What I learned instead was that our performance for family and friends invited applause and even brought people to their feet. In certain quarters, the Roccasalvo twins were the toast of Sheepshead Bay; henceforth, it was always Michael and Joseph, the conjunction *and* eliminating any filial estrangement. I had earned back my brother and my American citizenship.

A principle to which I adhere is that brilliance does not exist without shadows; they are correlative—what I call the defects of the quality. And so for all the affection I received from multiple caregivers, the experience had a dark side: an oscillation of now you have it, now you don't. True, it often felt like a paradise of provision, but the inconstancy proved as strong as the pampering; it vanished in the recess of memory and resurfaced as yearning. Heidegger was right when he wrote: "The past is with us as having-been." I offer one example:

In 1974, after being approved for the priesthood, I experienced a strong resistance to ordination. Toward the end of the spring semester, my brother Michael had visited me at Harvard and announced he was leaving the Jesuit order. Plans to be ordained together were null and void. The decision so churned the waters that his waves inundated my shore. I felt completely at sea. So I put ordination off and disguised my quandary by quipping to friends, "Always a bridesmaid, never a bride." It was a dark interlude in a bright year of study.

The summer was free of commitments except for August when I planned to visit a friend in the Basque Country. In the interim, I sought advice to deal with my indecision by arranging sessions with Dr. Bernard Hall, a psychiatrist on Central Park South.

"Why are you here?" he asked during our first meeting.

"I need help in resolving a conflict. I'm having doubts about being ordained."

"Tell me about yourself. Start anywhere you like."

So it began. He listened to the colorful rendition of my early childhood—what I call my infancy narrative. The tone was facetious and belied my feelings. I had yet to learn that my lighthearted manner was a defense mechanism against anxiety. Dr. Hall heard my story but said nothing. That he was not amused should have alerted me; he had bypassed the humor to listen for something deeper. After that session and several others, I started to feel I was repeating myself.

One afternoon, after a therapy session, I took the train to Brooklyn to be with my parents. When I arrived, I learned that my mother had already left to visit my great-aunt, Antoinette, and the Greek woman, Christina, who shared her household. Mother was asked to settle a disagreement. Two old women fixed in their ways refused to adjust their habits. Mutual respect had yielded to quarrels and name-calling. Mother would adjudicate the situation by playing prosecutor and defense attorney, for she was superb at seeing both sides to arrive at reconciliation. She planned to be home for dinner by five. Meanwhile, I found myself alone with my father—a welcome occurrence since he was often occupied with clients.

It was a lovely summer day, I recall, when the sun and the breezes from Sheepshead Bay invited an afternoon stroll. My father and I walked to Manhattan Beach while observing along the way the manorial homes and gated estates. We ambled back to the Varuna Boat Club where he was a member. Side by side, we leaned against the railing and watched the boats coming into harbor weighed down with their catch. No doubt the squid, lobster, and crab would be on display at Randazzo's Fish Market where Mother bought flounder for one of her signature meals.

We left the bay front, and after buying items for dinner, my father and I returned home before five. I set the table for three and got a head start on dinner: I put together a tossed salad, steamed some green beans, and warmed the cutlets left over from an earlier meal. By five twenty, my mother had still not arrived, and I saw my father beginning to pace. He walked to the bedroom window that looked out on Ocean Avenue. Craning his neck to see if Mother was near, he left the window in disappointment. At a quarter to six, he was back again but made no effort to hide his anxiety.

"Where's your mother?" he muttered.

He wasn't expecting an answer, so I said nothing. I kept myself busy in the kitchen while his fretful mood played on my nerves. It was now after six, and he repeated the question "Where's your mother?" like a mantra.

At first dismissible, the question began to rattle me. My father's futile attempt to control his agitation had me panicked. My hands tingled and my stomach groaned. But it was my mind that lost its balance, for I had imagined a sequence of horrors. When at six twenty my mother walked in, she apologized for her lateness by offering a reasonable explanation:

"I had to fill two prescriptions for Antoinette and Christina. Instead of having them ready, the pharmacist kept me waiting. And I phoned him earlier to say I was coming."

Her words returned my father to his Sicilian reserve, while I still oscillated between relief and exhaustion.

Two days later, I was sitting with Dr. Hall.

"How are you?" he asked.

"Fine," I said with a pause he must have noted.

"Anything you want to mention?"

"Well, something did happen on Friday. It was stupid and I overreacted. It's probably nothing."

"Tell me about it," he said.

In repeating my story, I focused on my father and exempted myself from the scene. Hall noted the omission and addressed it.

"During your father's uneasiness, what were you feeling?"

"Anxiety. My mother was supposed to be home by five. She did not arrive till after six. My father's repeated question about my mother's whereabouts triggered a reaction. I was in a state of panic."

"What were you thinking?"

"She had vanished for good."

"Anything else?"

"Yes. I felt her absence was a way of punishing me."

"What had you done?"

"I spent time with my father."

"Why was she punishing you for being with your father?"

"I don't know. But I felt sure she was."

"Why were you sure?"

"My mother is reliable. She's never late. The question 'Where's your mother?' tested that belief."

"Do you hear what you're saying?"

"Hear what?"

"Your question."

"It was my father's."

"You made it your own. Why did you?"

"I don't know, do you?"

"What I know doesn't count. It's what you know that matters."

"Then you know and won't tell me?"

Dr. Hall did not answer but looked at his watch. It was ten minutes to the hour.

"The session is over."

"Am I supposed to leave here with no answer?"

"Go out and live."

"How can I? I'm in a fog."

His buzzer sounded for the next client.

"I'll see you Friday," he said.

I left his office cursing my dependence on him. Instead of answering the question, "Where's your mother?" I was saddled with another, "What's the connection?" I resented Hall's unwillingness to share what he knew. It was mid-August and I had one final session with him. I decided next time to press him for clarity before I left for Europe.

The following Friday my therapy ended. What I recall of that session were Dr. Hall's parting remarks:

"I never terminate a client. If something troubling comes up, you're welcome to return."

"What about my question?"

"Put it to the side of your eyes. In time you may find clarity. What I said still stands. Go out and live." With that recommendation, I left him.

The following week, I found myself on the Atlantic coast in St. Jean de Luz. It wasn't long before I joined my Harvard friend, his wife, and her family. But before meeting up with them, I did sightseeing during the day and walked along the shore at night. It was unseasonable for August, so I bundled up against the chill wind. As the waves licked my heels, I remembered lines from Matthew Arnold's poem, "Dover Beach." I too was "on a darkling plain" and heard the ocean's "long, withdrawing, melancholy roar." It repeated the same question, "Do you hear what you're saying?" Evenings alone heightened my isolation, made more acute by the bleak Atlantic. Along that coast, I grasped the meaning of loneliness. My friends arrived just in time to distract me. There were picnics and dinners, wine and food enhanced by conversation. I was back to the house around the corner, to its warmth and affection. For the time being, I forgot my question.

In early September, I flew back to Boston and took up residence in Cambridge. I was happy to return to graduate study, to the mastery of Buddhist doctrine and to my efforts at finding a doctoral topic. The only interruption—and a welcome one—was a visit from my mother who was eager to see Harvard and share my university life. During the last week of September, she stayed at my apartment for a three-day weekend, arriving on Friday and leaving on Monday. I had bought tickets for the theater and planned several dinners out. She and I enjoyed our time together like friends meeting after separation.

I do not know what possessed her one night to speak of my infancy. Had she sensed a question at the side of my eyes? We had gone to a one-act drama and dined at a restaurant known for attracting student clientele. She had enjoyed the play immensely, and at dinner kept up a lively flow of conversation. She repeated a story about her undergraduate years at NYU, how she had been one of the Washington Square Players. She recounted her role in a Pirandello play where an onion on stage had helped her weep profusely. Mother summarized the plot: she was being forced by her father to marry a cousin in order to unite their two families. One scene required copious crying as she pleaded with her father to cancel the wedding. An onion she squeezed furtively in her eyes produced the requisite tears that streamed down her face. This doleful outburst had her director marveling in the wings. How she got rid of the onion by leaving it on a chair; how it clung to her father when he sat on it; how she grabbed at the onion hanging from his pants by pursuing him around the stage provoked a riot of laughter. Melodrama had turned into comedy long before TV mastered the transition. At the restaurant, she had us both laughing at her theatrical antics. She delighted in her role as comedian even when performing for an audience of one.

During the walk to my building, she was still enjoying her trip down memory lane. Once in my apartment, as she prepared for bed, she advanced to my infancy keeping up the same humorous tone. Something in her version—how my grandparents worshiped me and would not give me up; how I was always being hugged or held; how I cried for Pina when I finally returned home—sounded strained. I waited for a pause. Then without warning I said: "Why did you give me away?"

I still hear her voice coming from the room's dimly lit corner. Her words, though steady, were filled with emotion, for she spoke the truth as she knew it.

"I always loved you, Joseph. I missed you terribly, more than I can say. But I didn't have the strength to handle two babies."

The answer to the question "Where is your mother?" came to me in a room full of shadows. She had bowed to circumstances beyond her control and given me up. I did not challenge the facts; they had the ring of realism. I felt sad and forgiving all at once. I walked over to where Mother stood and saw she was crying. I said nothing but held her till the tears subsided.

"It's been quite a day," I said. "We've earned our rest."

Years later when I read her entries for 1941-42, I found confirmed what she told me in Cambridge. There I had heard the truth in person. Now I held it in a diary.

Analysis of the past has taught me that I'm drawn to those who are orphaned. In fact, it's mutual: we have an instinct for finding one another. An orphan is defined as a person bereft of parents. The loss has resulted from death, disappearance, abandonment, or desertion. Parental separation creates characters that are self-contained and introspective. At home with their solitude, they strive at all costs for affection. Metaphorically, life is a journey of self-understanding; its purpose, to uncover one's roots and forge a self-identity. A recurrent theme is the mentor relationship between a sage figure, male or female, and the orphaned boy or girl coming of age who seeks guidance. When compelled to leave home, orphans become displaced persons. If they cross international borders by forced migration, they are refugees, for the new cultural and linguistic environment is alien to the place of origin.

It's clear to me the word *orphan* applies, though not in the strictest sense. From the involuntary replacement of my immediate family with an adopted one to my speaking a foreign language, the concept proves relevant. So too the role of mentor: whether parish priests, Jesuits at school, or Harvard professors, the search for guides prevailed. My novels and short stories confirm the connection. When I examine them for structure and meaning, invariably the plots involve a death, a disappearance, or some familial loss, while a sage figure of religious background guides the protagonist through the crisis. I see my literary inventions as a repetitive exercise in which I'm retrieving my past and resolving it. Evelyn Waugh once said that novelists, whether they know it or not, have only one story to tell. Everything they concoct is a variation on a single theme. Mine is an imaginary effort to deal with yearning. Whether I'm being deadly serious, ironic, or indulging in buffoonery, my favorite stance is compassionate irony, what I like to call serious fun. Such ambiguity means keeping one foot in and one foot out; being in touch yet staying a touch remote; in Forster's lapidary phrase of the poet Cavafy, of "standing at a slight angle to the universe."

English is rich in synonyms for desire. One may hanker for money or covet power; crave wealth or long for security; look for sex or hunger for a meal; thirst for a drink or pine for a country. But yearning like anxiety is objectless. It is a state of mind whose intensity is in proportion to some prior bereavement. The temptation persists to return to the trauma and fix it; to search out persons who dramatize the loss and make it right. The compulsion to repeat is stronger when the object of love withholds itself. Reluctance is viewed as enhancing the value, not for any innate quality but for some projected excellence. We pursue the elusive object like the mythical Tantalus who cranes for fruit that hangs within reach but always eludes his grasp. The lyrics from a song say it well: "Maybe this time I'll win." "What" you may ask "is the sought for prize?" Trust as enduring love. Yeats disqualified any success in its pursuit when he wrote that "Man is in love and loves what vanishes—what else is there to say?" His is not the final word.

I find solace in Christianity's ability to heal the past. It is present in Jesus's parable of the prodigal son, of the transient boy returning home to his father who searches the horizon for his lost child. Had Jesus recounted this one tale, he would have earned a place in the annals of short story tellers. The image of God as compassionate parent—the maternal father—is incomparable. Here is my rendition:

The Prodigal Son
(Luke 15:11-32)

Of two sons, one was misguided.
The father, in whom he confided,
Was told, "Not yet heir,
Still I want my half share
Of the assets you've duly divided."

In an instant the boy took up travel
To cities where morals unravel.
He lived without want
As a rich bon vivant,
Though his spirit was sifting like gravel.

In opulent villas he'd crash,
For his money was making a splash.
His dissolute life
You could cut with a knife,
Then pleasure gave out with the cash.

A famine had put him in need,
So he hired himself out to feed
A bevy of pigs,
Whose corn pods and sprigs
Made him wake up and finally take heed.

"My own father's workmen have bread
And a sheltering roof overhead,
While I'm without digs

And still mired with pigs—
I'm sulking again, enough said.

I'll return to my family anew
And say 'Father, I've sinned against you.
Though what's done is done,
To call myself son
Is to state what is plainly untrue.'"

So he tramped across valleys and farms,
And arrived quite bereft of his charms.
In typical fashion
The father's compassion
Embraced him with wide open arms.

Embarrassed, the son would have rather
Been shunted aside than to bother
And say how chagrined
He now felt, having sinned,
Before heaven, the world, and his father.

Intent on a simple command,
The father gave no reprimand:
"For my son, robe and sandal,
Not a word more of scandal,
Let's eat, drink, and strike up the band.

My son who was lost has been found,
Though I feared him ten feet underground.
It's fitting and right

This auspicious night
To fête him like one laurel-crowned."

In the fields slaved the son's older brother.
(It's amazing they had the same mother.)
His militant poise
Couldn't cope with the joys
Of people who'd found one another.

Approaching the house, he was burning.
He stopped at the door and was churning:
"To think this elation,
And sham celebration
Result from a hustler's returning."

The father's attempts at amends
He dismissed as loose odds and ends:
"Five years and a half,
And not once was a calf
Ever roasted for me and my friends.

Meanwhile this wastrel of yours,
Depleted by drink, drugs and whores,
From out of the blue
Returns home to you
And drags himself in on all fours.

He's robbed, mugged, cheated, and lied
And abdicates all sense of pride.
I've reason to shun

This tramp you call son—
No, I'll never join you inside."

Having let his son's anger subside,
Drawing near him, the father replied:
"What's mine is all yours,
In peacetime and wars,
Compassion be ever your guide.

By taking your lost brother's part,
I proved myself true from the start.
To sons, lost or found,
I'm paternally bound
To be boundless in soul, mind and heart."

At the risk of doctrinal dross,
Permit one marginal gloss:
How Jesus, the prodigal,
Was highly methodical
In squandering himself on the cross.

This tale of a profligate brother
Assures like a nurturing mother;
So feel the mortality
Of Christ's prodigality:
Be lavish in loving each other.

I receive a comparable solace whenever I view the Buddha, whose knowing smile embraces all in its aura of peace. In metal or stone I find the same affirmation: compassion is at the heart of the universe.

iii

It is time for me to focus on my mother Lucie, who till now has played an important yet sporadic role in this memoir. I begin with the eulogy I gave at her funeral on July 14, 2005. It is a portrait of her in miniature that offers a framework for enlargement.

Eulogy

It's hard to believe she's gone, our mother, Lucie. Our memories of her have such verve and vigor: the quick intelligence, the goals that seemed a foregone conclusion, and the resourcefulness that seamlessly matched means to end. We asked ourselves how this colossus of femininity could ever be stopped, for she outlived them all: eleven brothers and sisters. We thought she might—just to prove she could—outlive us too. Under my breath I walked away from her saying, "Lucie is still juicy."

Who of us could forget how she came to the ten thirty Mass on Sundays a few minutes late; how at the confession of faults she made her entrance down the nave on her walker, then turned to announce to the church—as if they didn't know—"That's my son, the priest."

Who of us could forget how she took over the piano in the parlor to play songs from the forties: "It Had To Be You" and "Melancholy Baby."

She always ended with "Santa Lucia" just to make sure you knew who was playing. Lucie was like that, clear about who she was even to the spelling of her name. I wrote a limerick about it:

To family and friends she was LUCIE,

Like the anglicized sound of Debussy;

But miffed she would be

If instead of IE,

You used the Y-ending of Lucy.

We used to smile when we saw her with Dr. Isadore Gilman, another nonagenarian, and how sweet they were on each other. Lucie turned a man's head, even if he had to shift in his wheelchair to do it. Before Isadore there was Jacob, a Columbia psychoanalyst; and before Jacob, my father, a medical masseur and physiotherapist. She preferred professional healers.

Linguist, poet, short story writer, essayist, and PTA playwright: to whatever she set her mind it was achieved. But she knew when to accept the inevitable and bow to circumstance. In her last thirty years she nursed two Michaels, our father and brother, through severe illness. Never once did she veer from her resolve to care for them. Resourceful and intelligent, yes, but she was loyal to a fault. If you were admitted to her friendship, you became family.

In her 1930 diary—one of thirty volumes amounting to eight thousand pages—the following sentence occurs: "I am lucky in that I do not possess many friends." My sister Joan and I could not disagree more. Despite her manner of sometimes appearing remote and keeping her own counsel, she did possess friends. Her generosity of spirit attracted them and drew them into her intimacy. Then she became their advocate: taxes, court cases, doctors' visits, alimony, she was always there, her energy on tap.

There was a shadow side to her brilliance, the defect of her qualities, for she could shun an inconstant friend or dispose of a treacherous enemy.

To protect her own she was like a tigress. It came with the territory: the red hair and hazel eyes, the Ricci side sparring with the Martella. There was no fury like Lucie scorned, and I ran for cover when her volcanic rage erupted.

Yet the image that lingers is of her sitting with a book in one hand and a diploma in the other. I hear her saying to Joan, Michael, and me: "You have to have latitude and longitude of vision," as she gestured with both hands to shape the globe. She proved it by sending the three of us to Jewish vacation camps. We went to Shabbat services on Friday and learned to sing and pray in Hebrew years before Pius XII called Christians "spiritual Semites." Intolerant of intolerance, she valued diversity. She made me a comparative religionist long before Harvard, and my sister's degrees in music and theology are proof Lucie got her way.

So in these last months, it was hard for us to watch her dwindle as she refused her glasses and hearing aids. She waved them off and relied on the one thing she trusted along with her intellect: her sense of touch. On separate days when Joan and I sat beside her, her eyes focused on us like some icon of the Mother of God. She gazed and did not blink. Suddenly she tugged at us, pulled us close, and kissed us saying, "I love you from the bottom of my heart," then sealed her words with the sign of the cross. The veil of the temple had been rent in two and we were given a glimpse of her holy of holies. Lucie indeed: *lux ex luce,* so our profession of faith goes, "light from light."

Since Tuesday, we've thought how her going is a gift and her absence, a gain. We've thought: "While we do without, won't her two Michaels be pleased." It seems a fair exchange. It was a blessing not to watch her languish, for that was never her style. In her declining years, Lucie had tasted something of heaven; now she wanted the real thing. That's why she met death calmly, deliberately, gracefully, for she entered with open eyes.

Decades before, she had entered the world with closed eyes on December 13, 1906. Born on the feast of St. Lucy, she was named Lucia Anita, the fifth child of Francesco Martella and Camilla Ricci. Here are lapidary portraits of my maternal grandparents.

Francesco Martella was born in 1871 to Loredo Martella and Maria di Maria in San Severo, a commune of Vico Gargano in Puglia, Italy. On the certificate of citizenship—he was naturalized in 1934 at the age of sixty-two—he is described as having gray hair, a height of five foot ten inches, and a weight of 175 pounds. In his photo he is wearing a summer suit, white shirt, and dark tie with a tie bar; he sports a short mustache and resembles in his sixties the German writer, Thomas Mann. My grandfather's address is given as 2640 East Eleventh Street, Brooklyn. He lived until 1958 when he died at age eighty-six.

I have a picture of him in his twenties after he had come down to Rome and become a *carabiniere,* an officer in the Roman police force. Looking in his youth like Ronald Coleman, and sporting his signature mustache, he's handsome in his dark blue uniform. He is standing with his left hand gripping his sword and his right hand holding a plumed helmet. His jacket has epaulettes and two rows of gold buttons running parallel down the front. Slender, dashing, a ladies' man, I can see why my grandmother was attracted to him. He never lost the erect posture, broad gait, and swagger as he entered a room.

What I remember most about him was the weekly visit to our home. He carried a cane with a silver handle and wore two crucifix rings: a platinum one on the fourth finger of his left hand, and one in gold on the fourth finger of his right. I replicated the one in gold on my last trip to Rome, and I wear it on occasion to remember him. The crucifix rings came as no surprise since he was a deeply religious man. My mother told me that he was orphaned early and raised by priests. Did he attend the Palazzo del Seminario in San Severo? Was he taught by Benedictines whose church was built by monks from Montecassino? Either case is arguable. In the basement of the house on Eleventh Street was an altar populous with saints and full of votive candles. I was told Grandpa would go through the rubrics of Mass for any major feast. He was schooled in the Latin liturgy before it became vernacularized by Vatican II.

His Tuscan Italian was impeccable with no trace of regional accent. He cited from memory the Gospel of the given Sunday, and I recall his use of the *passato remoto* verb forms—difficult for their irregularity—which rolled off his tongue: *"E dunque Gesù disse"* ("And then Jesus said . . ."). His spoken speech was formally elegant, quite different from Grandma Martella's Italian, which she spoke in her regional dialect. Once when someone was knocking at the front door—a sound my mother had missed—Grandpa turned and said to her: *"Lucia, vedi chi picchia a la porta"*; which translated is best rendered, "Lucy, see who's rapping at the door." His sons, my uncles, got hold of the verb for "knocking," and pranced about saying *"pichia, pichia."*

He was thrilled to learn I planned to study for the priesthood, for I was finishing what he had left unfinished. It was said he should have stayed in the seminary. His umbrella business was never successful; for days he disappeared from his family and a wife who was invariably pregnant. He never practiced family planning, and my grandmother at age fifty-one gave birth to my aunt Rosie who became the youngest in the family. If the Ricci side had not intervened to help my grandmother start a grocery store, the family would have been indigent. As it was, three girls as teenagers left home to marry unsuccessfully, and one uncle proved so delinquent he was incarcerated until his adulthood. Grandpa never lived to see me in Jesuit black for he died in 1958 at eighty-six. It was my graduation day from Brooklyn Prep, so my brother and I had no party out of respect for his passing. My mother came to our commencement in funereal black, and hovered between sadness at his death and pride at our success.

I always remember him as a *galantuomo*, with his focused gaze standing tall under the grape arbor in his backyard. He was a financial disappointment to his family and wife from whom he separated in later years—he went to live with a daughter and she with a son—but he never lost his self-esteem. To my commercially astute Sicilian grandfather who liked to talk of money (*i soldi*), Grandpa Martella gave his customary reply: *"Magari sono povero, ma io sono romano"*; "I may be poor but I'm Roman." What did poverty matter when Grandpa could claim Roman citizenship? That urban attribute was priceless and ensured under any circumstance his superiority.

Born in 1878, Camilla Ricci was one of five children of Michele Ricci and his wife, Lapicirella. Grandma's youngest sister, Antoinette, was my mother's patron and advocate. It was from her I learned I was the second in the family to join the Jesuits, the first being Matteo Ricci. As a young priest of twenty-six, he set out for the Far East in 1578. He produced the first global map that revolutionized Chinese understanding of the world. By 1589 he was sharing mathematical ideas with Chinese scholars and was renowned for his memory and knowledge of astronomy. He mastered spoken and written Mandarin and published several volumes on morality, mathematics, and a treatise on friendship. In Beijing there is a small temple in which you will find entombed Li Matou, the only foreigner the Chinese say helped them understand their nation.

Ricci was born in Macerata in central Italy and capital of the province in the Marche region. It is possible that Grandma's family came from that city. My aunt Antoinette was never clear on origins, whether familial or geographic. My knowledge of Macerata came from another resident, the oriental scholar Giuseppe Tucci; he had pioneered excavations from Iran to Tibet, and I used his Italian translations of Tibetan Buddhism while at Harvard. I rendered them into English to the delight of my Japanese mentor whose prodigious knowledge of languages did not include Italian.

The other Ricci besides Matteo whom Antoinette mentioned was Ruggiero, the violin prodigy; his early genius flowered into a performance career of over 5,000 concerts in sixty-five countries. He is known for having the widest repertoire of any living violinist, and his recording of Paganini's Caprices on the composer's Guarneri violin has become normative. He was my mother's second cousin. My sister and I tried without luck to visit him in Salzburg, Austria, where he taught at the Mozarteum. He now lives in Palm Springs, and though he no longer gives concerts, he acts as mentor for gifted violinists.

Grandma Martella was no celebrity Ricci like Matteo or Ruggiero, but she was a luminary in my eyes. Her certificate of citizenship says she was fifty-five when she became naturalized in 1933, with dark brown hair and eyes, small in stature—five foot five inches—with a full figure that broadened because of so many childbirths. She had that exhausted, startled look of someone who never rested. I never saw her laugh though she smiled sweetly. But she was a brilliant storyteller. My fondest memories are when my mother and father left for an evening and Grandma "baby sat." My brother and I were allowed to sleep in my parents' bed, while she told us stories in her accented and slightly broken English. I learned later during graduate studies that she drew on a stock of tales recited not only bedside, but also hearthside during medieval pilgrimage. While reading *The Canterbury Tales*, I had a déjà vu; I had heard them many times before.

When she thought we were asleep, she would remove the combs from her hair. Once I awoke and saw her graying locks cascade below her waist. I can still hear the soft electricity as she combed her crowning glory. She braided her hair with great dexterity winding it this way and that; it sat on her head like a coronet while she smoothed a stray lock in place. In the morning Michael and I took turns sitting on her lap pressed against her corpulence. In my naughtiness I hit the hanging flesh of her arms and watched it quiver, only to hear her say sweetly, *"Giuseppino, lasciami sola, favore"*; "Little Joseph, leave me alone, please." I think she enjoyed the attention. She died in 1968 at the age of ninety. The brief obituary says it well: "Camilla Martella, beloved mother, and sister of Antoinette Ricci."

My mother Lucie was first to be born in the United States. Mary, Louie, Mike, and Paul had all preceded her, and Mother was yet to be followed by Rachel, Yetta, Louise, Tony, Nicky, and Rosie; in all, eleven brothers and sisters. A twelfth was informally adopted, my cousin Frankie, who was the child of my uncle Louie. My maternal grandmother was thirty-one when she gave birth to my mother and fifty-one when she had my aunt Rosie. The story circulated that my grandfather disappeared for weeks to pursue his umbrella business and then returned to find a new child. While the story may have no basis in fact, its intent was to criticize his casual link to paternity. They said Grandpa Martella was better at making children than earning money whose scarcity amounted to borderline poverty. Multiple offspring living in cramped quarters led to bickering and made privacy impossible. Invidious comparisons about who received more food at meals or wore better clothes plagued my mother's early years. Her loyalty was stretched to the elastic limit between family and higher learning, yet she dutifully embraced both, studying with a child on one knee and a college text on the other. What money she made as stenographer at the telephone company she gave to support the family, for she worked during the day and took courses at night. She often spoke of how she scrimped on food and made a meal of coffee and animal crackers to have money for books. Deprivation accounts for that remote, dreamy look in her early photos. Longing to escape her family, she became a regular at Hollywood movies. Their glamour helped her envision a world of celebrity in which fame and fortune would finally be hers. Ambition, hard work, and success—these are the recurrent words in her 1930 diary. Despite the looming depression, she had reasons to believe she could achieve her goals. Gifted with an expansive mind that had a flair for mathematics and literature, she had an equal talent for dramatic performance. That she was slender with deep auburn hair, pale skin, amber eyes, and a ready wit made her an enchanting companion. What I later recognized as "Bette Davis eyes" was a certain Renaissance hauteur. It was the imperious gaze of a Medici portrait that probed the spectator. In those moments of assessment, Mother discerned if she would be your friend. It was a title she rarely bestowed. In her diary she speaks of friendship and how she construes it. She writes:

> Our best friends bring out the best, not in a narrow puritanical sense of course, but best as regards mutual pleasures and interests and works. Many of us waste time and energy and means with people who are boring to us and to whom we are in turn probably boring—simply from the lack of a little analysis and planning. There should be nothing calculating about friendship.

If ever you sought her help, she gave it generously, for her resourcefulness seldom missed its mark. But she never allowed advocacy to be mistaken for friendship. Once her work was finished and your gratitude was expressed, she would quietly steal away. From time to time I heard her repeat the adage, "intimacy breeds contempt." She never questioned its veracity, and she never applied it to friends. She said she was "lucky" in possessing a few, but she had them for life. Listen to what she wrote of two women she loved dearly:

Emily McCart is the dearest, sweetest friend I have; five years
friendly and never a quarrel: the dearest and sweetest friend.
Anna Munno is someone regarding whom my feelings change
quite often. She is so changeable herself. I like her immensely.
She is a very good companion, very bright with a good mind;
13 years friendly, many quarrels, but we still like each other's
company.

Meticulous about remembering their birthdays, anniversaries, and
special occasions, she lost access to friends only when distance or death
severed the connection. Because she lived in an age without computers,
cell phones, fax machines, or BlackBerries, friends needed to be close.
Proximity was everything.

If friendship was central to my mother's life, so was education. It
began at PS 168 on First Avenue at 317 East 104th Street. Since my
grandparents and their children lived on East 111th, it was an easy walk
each day. The elementary school opened its doors in 1910, four years
after Mother's birth, so her attendance from 1912 through 1920 was at a
new institution. The building, newly roofed, is still there but it has since
been converted into apartments.

I have a picture of Mother's graduation dated of June 1920. In the
foreground is the U.S. flag exhibiting forty-eight stars for the (then) states
of the union. Lucie stands at the photo's center, her shoulder length hair
in long curls. She wears a white filet around her forehead in the style of
the time which kept hair back from the face. John Crowe Ransom in his
poem, "Blue Girls," tells his seminary class of adolescents: "Tie the white
filets then about your hair/And think no more of what will come to pass."
Mother disregarded such advice; she alone holds her diploma perfectly
vertical. Doubtless, she would have brandished it like Joan of Arc's sword

despite her classmates standing left and right. Lying in the crux of her arm is the requisite bouquet of flowers. The look on her face is focused. She seems to be planning her rise to the echelons of academe.

She next went to Julia Richman High School located at 317 East Sixty-seventh Street. She earned a commercial degree in four years but stayed on for two more to graduate with an academic diploma. She never lost her skill using shorthand—Isaac Pitman, as I recall—and I still can't decipher her dots and tittles in an otherwise seamless sentence. In her diaries she broke into shorthand to write something meant for her eyes.

During Mother's secondary education, the family moved to 2640 East Eleventh Street in Brooklyn. My grandparents resided there till old age forced them to live with a son or daughter. She commuted to Manhattan to finish high school in 1926, and she graduated from Julia Richman with a command of Spanish. In 1923 her instructor, Helen Collins, gave her a book on the art of Seville inscribing it: *a Lucia Martella in testimonio de su afición al espagnol*. Mother admired Cervantes's *Don Quixote,* and in her 1930 diary named it together with Fielding's *Tom Jones* and Dante's *Divina Commedia,* one of her favorite books. Her Spanish edition was heavily annotated in her careful script. Seven decades later when she took a Spanish course at NYU, her instructor said she was the best in the class. At the time she was eighty-seven.

In 1926 she attended NYU's Washington Square College. As a member of the drama club, she played beleaguered heroines. She graduated in 1930 with a bachelor of science degree and a double major in math and Spanish. She demonstrated her love of numbers by later translating their primacy into Wall Street investments. Was it the certitude that dispelled ambiguity? Early mastery came with some misgivings. Here is a poem from 1926 in which she ventilates her anger at her math teacher. Aptly called, "A Song of Hate"; it exhibits her ease with verse, and this from one whose parents spoke only Italian:

Given just a triangle,
A figure of dimension,
Or maybe just a quadrangle
That causes such dissension.

Given this and given that
To prove what should not be;
Given all such tommyrot
And prove by QED.

What a bible of congestion
Is this geometric book!
Why it ruins my digestion
Just with one decided look.

And my hard-boiled math professor
With his polygonic smile,
Looks a guilty rum confessor
With his mathematic style.

"Given this, now prove me that!"
He scowls to the class.
"Given this, you've proved me what?"
Then sighs, "Alas, alas."

During the summer of 1928, after finishing sophomore year, she took a cruise to Havana accompanied by her close friend, Anna Munno. Her purpose may have been to broaden her conversational Spanish. Anna later became Mother's bridesmaid at her wedding in 1933. In the three photos

I have of her, Anna is a compelling presence with huge soulful eyes and a brilliant smile. Lucie and Anna are now standing on the ship's deck in white pleated skirts, arms interlocked; now they are lying in deck chairs enjoying the open sea. Anna's penmanship is as striking as her physical presence. In two messages to my mother her words are shaped by pressure on her pen's nib: "Lucy [sic]: I hope that from these books in cozy nooks you'll derive some pleasure during your hours of leisure." And in another: "Enjoying this book immensely. Will call you Saturday in regard to dance. No dates, remember! Anna."

Sometime during their Cuban holiday my mother met I. G. Valladares. I still have the business card he gave Mother over eighty years ago. I believe he fell in love with her during her holiday and may have asked her to marry him. That he never forgot her is clear from an incident occurring on March 26, 1938. Mother was already married five years, and my sister Joan was three years old. Valladares managed to commandeer time on Radio CMX, a Cuban station hailing from Havana. Mr. Richard J. Sutherland of Toledo, Ohio, had tuned in that morning at 1:25 a.m.; in a later message to the station he writes that "You asked one of your listeners in New York to call and give information to a Ms. Martella. At 1:29 a.m. a number was played that you said was a typical piece of Cuban music . . . 'Your beautiful eyes.' Your program came through fine with good volume and clarity. Wishing to continue my listening I will close. Respectfully yours, Richard J. Sutherland." The song's lyrics made famous by Dean Martin are addressed to a man's beloved: "You and your beautiful eyes/ That tell such beautiful lies/Well, they ought to give you a prize/You and your beautiful eyes." Why did Valladares in such a dramatic manner and after a ten year absence suddenly address this song to a "Ms. Martella"? He presumed she was still single. Was he also? Could he have been so smitten with Lucie that he carried a torch for a decade?

My mother insisted that Valladares had named a perfume after her which he called "Lucevan." Whether it remained in the planning stage or was ever produced I cannot say, but every effort to find it and inhale the maternal essence has been futile. Only recently did I decipher the perfume's name. "Lucevan" is a truncated form for the Italian, *lucevano*, which begins an aria in Pucini's opera, *Tosca*. The painter Cavaradossi has been sentenced to death for hiding an escaped political prisoner. As he awaits his fate, he sings of his beloved Tosca and his dashed dreams: *"E lucevan le stelle,/e olezzava la terra/stridea l'uscio dell'orto,/e un passo sfiorava la rena./Entrava ella, fragrante,/mi cadea fra le braccia"*; "And the stars shone brightly, the earth breathed perfume, a footstep brushed the sand path. She entered, fragrant, and fell into my waiting arms."

iv

Letter to My Mother

Dear Mother:

It seems strange to be addressing a letter to you when you're already deceased—it will be five years in July—but if I take faith seriously you're alive. Shortly after birth you were christened with hope at baptism, while before death you were anointed by rites steeped in the language of resurrection. Signed, sealed, and delivered into eternal life, you're no less a presence to me now than you were in the flesh. In fact you're more vivid, for I can visit with you any time, whereas before you were subject to the vagaries of age.

A realist who sees it otherwise might say I'm writing you under the pretense that your mind still functions; only then can I accept you as real. The same realist stresses my need:

"You write, Joseph, for your own comfort to recall the past and settle it. You're offering your mother a posthumous tribute. Her portrait will not be all sweetness and light, for you never tire of saying, 'There is no brilliance without shadow.' Those who remember Lucie as a beacon of clarity may object to any shading. Their viewpoint will not supplant your own. This letter is meant for her."

Mother, both religious and realist attitudes motivate me. Together they explain why I find you a vivifying presence. The thirty diaries you left are an admirable help. They run the gamut of sixty-seven years and occupy two shelves on my bookcase. Your memorabilia of essays, short stories, and poetry fill a third. I have more words of yours than time remaining; I'm forced to be selective. What interest me are your entries for 1930 and 1937 in which you set down your prior and subsequent marital reflections. Guided by the principle that origins are given once and for all, my purpose is to understand your dreams and aspirations. Were they challenged by fears, and if so, did you overcome them? Finally, how did your dreams and aspirations shape my own?

Your graduation from NYU on June 28, 1930, was celebrated at the Varese Garden on Ocean Parkway. The formal invitation reads: "Mr. and Mrs. Frank Martella cordially invite you to a Graduation Party given in honor of their daughter Lucie Martella." Honor, indeed, for you graduated with a bachelor of science degree, having majored in math and Spanish literature. You had the distinction of being the only family member to earn a college diploma. It's delightful to look at your sepia portraits where you're dressed in cap and gown; in one you look nonplussed at your success; in another the gaze is soulful as if you're weighing plans for a life you've already decided. So it appears in the diary you kept for 1930 at the age of twenty-four. It's composed of lists followed by commentary. Each list, preceded by the heading, "I would like to," is followed by the words, "know more," "see more," "hear more," "read more." Your avid curiosity for art, music, plays, and travel is matched by a desire for a room of your own, for more books, clothes, and privacy. You see these tangible benefits not as a source of happiness but the means to intensify it. What's clear from the following pages is that these acquisitions are possible if your ambitions succeed and are financially rewarded. You're weary of discord among your brothers and sisters, of struggling for an education, of domestic hardship where necessities are doled out meagerly. You want the abundant life of Hollywood where luxury is daily on tap.

Intent on accomplishing your goals, you're eager to remove impediments that thwart your purpose. You begin with your personality and are introspective to a fault. You examine surgically your best and worst qualities and determine how to enhance or eliminate them. "I wish to acquire patience, self-control, tolerance, a balance in mood and action, a fixed attitude that is not changeable." You admire "a sweet and loving disposition at all times, the will to get ahead and not being discouraged." You value especially intelligence, good conversation, and affection. You're keenly aware of your social gift to attract friends, for you exercise a sense of humor in witty remarks and an ability to entertain. You're scrupulously honest and immaculate about your person; economical too in knowing how to buy without waste. Your warmth is mitigated by a reticence that shields your affection from those you love. You lament losing your temper, being intolerant, criticizing people, being moody, argumentative, and hating easily. You regret being heartless to those you dislike and resist the conviction that you may be wrong. You deplore your spasmodic fits in overdoing things to offset your poor fate. Your candor is blunt, for you know yourself well.

Oscillation between self-worth and personal insecurity you owe to familial privation and to many siblings for whom you've become responsible. You have "a child on one knee and a book on the other." Moody and sensitive, you are given to bad dreams. Hollywood films solace you but sharpen your desire for escape. Your fatalism makes obstacles insurmountable and is destructive of ideals, even as you hanker for "a new life." In the contest between darkness and light, it's difficult to know which side will win. At the callow age of twenty-four, it's poignant to hear you speak in the past subjunctive as if life has eluded you:

> I have attempted to acquire success with no realization that
> I needed first the characteristics to do so and second the
> opportunities. Had I been in a different family surrounding,
> *I might have become* a great actress, musician, teacher, or
> business woman, for I possessed the ability and intelligence
> for any career but was forced to pick the least interesting—a
> struggling stenographer.

In your mind's eye some insights may yet outwit your fate. You plan to avail yourself of influential people who will further your ambition to be known. You will use any opportunity, however small, that leads to success. Power, position, and prestige ensure income and life's extravagances which you must have. Eventually you will marry an intelligent boy. (In a Freudian slip you wrote "book" and corrected it.) Your husband will please you by staying agile in mind and expanding his success, a word that appears with calculable regularity. You will restrict yourself to two children, first a girl and then a boy. You contemplate marriage only if you've not succeeded in acquiring an advanced position. Then you will select a mate who is your equal "in education and intelligence." Together you will tour the globe, and when travel becomes tedious, you will have your first child: a baby girl. You describe her as if you were looking back on her career: "She is clever, talented, and pursues the course in which I failed. She will become a professional woman marked by prestige, glory, and an estimable reputation." Together with an accomplished daughter, you want money, "lots of it," to do with as you please. With "an ambitious and successful husband" who will make you independent, you will be proud of being married. "In other words," you conclude, "I want so badly what I did not have all my life."

On July 9, 1933, you married. The account of the experience was not written until four years later on March 29, 1937. You give a detailed picture of the event: the gown you wore, the nuptial service at Our Lady of Solace Church where Father Martiriano accepted your marital vows. Your brother Paul is best man and Anna Munno, maid of honor. A convivial reception follows with Uncle Paul's band entertaining. Typically, you list the wedding gifts and how they will feature in your Brooklyn home at 1711 East Fifteenth Street.

Your honeymoon at the Cavalier Hotel in Virginia Beach is memorable. You cite the lovely surroundings and the rustic atmosphere you call "enchanting." You've left me the Western Union telegram sent from the hotel to Grandma and Grandpa Roccasalvo: "Arrived safely at Cavalier Hotel, Virginia Beach. Everything fine. Don't worry, Michael and Lucie." The hotel still operates as a resort. On its Web site, it looks quite different from the postcard you kept in remembrance. But it appears as you described it: enchanting.

More revealing than your remarks about being seasick, landing by boat, and meeting friendly Americans is a sepia photo; it verifies the maxim that a picture is worth a thousand words. The snapshot shows you and Dad seated on a bench while the surf rolls in behind you. With his arm around your left shoulder, he displays the look of someone deeply in love and profoundly satisfied. His expressive eyes are saying: "How lucky I am." You look happy, your face filled with promise for the future. You make a handsome couple, for you are flawlessly dressed in the height of 1930s fashion.

Dad is wearing cream-colored slacks, two-tone shoes—white with brown leather at the toes—and an open sport jacket. For all the informality, he sports a white shirt and dark tie. A clip with a center jewel keeps the tie in place. You are wearing a white pleated dress with spread collar and high heels with vertical and horizontal straps. With legs crossed, you are leaning affectionately into each other. Dad is suavely handsome. The photo confirms what I recall you saying: "Your father was so good-looking when I married him," and you do not exaggerate. He has brown wavy hair, blue eyes, and a strong athletic build. Your hands are folded demurely on your lap, and you offer the viewer a shy, winsome smile. What a picture of contentment. The mood continues when you're home from your honeymoon, and deepens further when Joanie is born in 1935. Despite the Depression and food lines queuing up on city blocks, you write:

> The home we share is a symbol of happiness and of mutual anticipation of each other's company. With baby Joan now a member of the family, we are a happy trio. She has added that certain completeness which was lacking heretofore, and has rendered spontaneity of charm and vivacity. God keep her safe for us as we love her dearly. Without her life would not be worth living. This book will someday be in her safekeeping as a remembrance of her parents' lives. To destroy it would be a great loss. May it be in safe hands always, no matter how time has elapsed.

Your description of marital bliss makes me nostalgic for what might have been. With the vision of hindsight, I feel pressed to speak in the past subjunctive: if only you and Dad had sustained the rapport of those early years with Joanie. What I remember instead is strife.

After reading your diaries, I grasp why the rift between you and Dad became irreparably wide. Looking back after five decades, I see how abrasive events make the outcome inevitable. You are not prepared for a multiple birth. You planned for one boy, not twins, and the prolonged labor of giving birth has depleted you. Is it postpartum depression? If so, you never call it that. You are anemic, irritable, and underweight. In the infancy photos, you seem older than your thirty-four years. Your face

is grim—you never smile—and shadows are under your eyes. You seem
barely present. If you take pride in giving the Roccasalvos sons to ensure
the name, there's little pleasure in it for you. The daily grind of nursing two
babies whose needs are rarely synchronized is relentless. You appear on
the verge of exhaustion. Not the life you envisioned as a college graduate,
you call it what it is: "drudgery."

The proximity of the Martellas to the Roccasalvos offers some
advantage; both sides help with the babies. But it has its defects. Discord
continues among your sisters and brothers while Dad's parents prefer his
well-being to yours. Primogeniture dictates protocol: he's first their son
and secondly your husband. He never reverses the order and so is never
fully your partner. Joanie's scarlet fever requires hospitalization while
Michael's colicky behavior at night keeps you walking the floor. Without
relief you're at your wits' end for you cannot cope. From desperation you
surrender me to Grandma and Pina.

Did something else occur to deepen the crisis? Did dreams of an
affluent life return to haunt you? Are you aware of the gap between the
hopes of the 1930 diary and what transpires after? I think you are for you
escape into movies to relieve the pressure. You see several over a month
and fantasize on the world they enjoy. It's not yours. The Depression may
have passed, but Pearl Harbor occurs followed by the declaring of war and
the rationing of food. Life is pinched and the recurrent verb on your lips
is "economize." Dad's income, a pittance by your standards, heightens
the frustration. He works hard but the fruits of his labor are insufficient.
That he does not advance quickly proves he's not ambitious enough, and
he cannot ensure the abundance you want. Affection for him dries up.

"Lucie," I hear him say, "you're never satisfied."

That satisfaction comes in successive years as your children give
you what your marriage does not. Grades and medals, scholarships and
degrees—they're all compensatory. Your love for us runs deep, but it

never feels unconditional. There's an agenda to meet and ambitions to realize. We three must rise to the top of the heap for therein lies your definition as Mother. As purveyors of your dreams, we have the talents to fulfill them.

One example stands out in relief. I recall how Joanie is not awarded the General Excellence at her graduation from St. Mark's primary school. It's given to Patricia McKenna—I still recall the interloper's name. You react to this slight as if it was your own, and you rant and rave at the injustice. The anger is volcanic but it subsides. Not till years later when I graduate from St. Mark's with the coveted medal are you vindicated; justice has been done and the wrong rectified. The demands on me to make good the loss have been oppressive, but I win through to the end and am awarded the medal. You beam with pride. Success is what matters. It cannot be otherwise, for it results from tenacity, superiority, and recognition. Your children have what it takes for you're the Mother. With a purpose for living, you're filled with indomitable energy. The methodology is clear. Joanie must have piano lessons and go to private secondary school, while Michael and I share scholarships at the best Brooklyn high school run by the Jesuits. To meet ancillary costs, you teach pupils at home and return to work as executive secretary. It's stenography again but freely chosen. Your involvements range from PTA president to investor in the stock market. You're a veritable dynamo who in modern parlance balances home with career.

Joanie's decision to "enter the convent" fractures your plans. You quarrel with her and challenge her choice, but finally agree to her going. Her absence grieves you, and I recall how you sob uncontrollably whenever you visit her vacant bedroom. Years later she will meet the demands of your marital diary by earning degrees in musicology and the arts and two PhD's in distinct fields. The awards arrive late in a form you least expected. But they arrive.

And where is Dad during all this high drama? His status as Father has contracted till he becomes a virtual presence. I can only guess what he felt. You write in your 1930 diary that you bemoan your ability to be heartless. I think Dad felt the edge of your indifference for you punish by being remote. It's the shading in your personality that refuses to correct what is thought incorrigible. You press on, no matter what, and transcend whatever thwarts your purpose. I would have felt fatherless had the Jesuits not intervened. As a group, they are everything you admire in male intelligence. Their presence saves me from being orphaned a second time for I identify with them. Cumulatively they play Dad's role and receive the parental esteem I owed to him. I've since realized that I *am* my father's son. And if I could address him face-to-face, I would borrow the words of Augustine spoken to that Source from which all fatherhood comes: "Late have I loved you." My winning manner is his gift to me, though in my adolescence I recall the shame at his powerlessness in dealing with his family and in not getting the order right. If only he had said to them: "Now look, either you see my wife as first in my life or you stop seeing me." But he never confronts them since by nature he's conciliatory. His goodness which does not challenge galls you. If yours is Hebraic justice, his is Gospel benevolence. With the advance of time the mismatch becomes irreversible. Though your marriage remains intact, it's no longer a willed commitment but détente.

What an unenviable position in which to find myself: I am pressed to take sides. I take yours against his and intervene when I should have kept my counsel. I become the boy savior, a role not unlike the one I have as priest. I still intervene in the lives of those who are emotionally orphaned. It's uncanny how we find each other. By releasing the pheromone of intuitive insight, someone in need picks up the scent.

In summary, Mother, something remote from anything you intended has come out of my childhood, and out of the domestic turbulence in which I played a part; something neither you nor I could ever have imagined:

the polymorphic identity of priest, novelist, comparative religionist, and pedagogue. It proves again the Portuguese proverb: "God writes straight with crooked lines." Nothing is wasted since there's nothing of no moment. It's the divine brilliance casting its shadow a pace or two ahead of us.

This is a good time to end my letter. I promise to use the epistolary form whenever direct address to you is preferable. From your privileged position you know what I've written is prompted by that truth and love in whose presence you live, move, and have your being.

V

It is clear to the reader that the Society of Jesus, the most humanistic order in the Catholic Church, was central to my teenage years. To bolster this truth, I can do no better than begin with James Hanley. I was fourteen when I met him. He was my freshman teacher of Latin and Religion at Brooklyn Prep, a Jesuit high school where I had won a scholarship during the entrance exam competition. I recall my first assembly in the school gym, how the headmaster, Fr. J. Vincent Watson, strode down the makeshift aisle. Standing before a stationary mike, he read aloud the names in eight freshman classes. The scholastics—seminarians in vows but not yet priests—took possession of the assigned groups of thirty-five students, and led them out.

Jim brought us to our homeroom, introduced himself, and distributed the reading list. The text I remember from constant use—and still have on my bookshelf—was Henle's *Latin Grammar. Caesar's Gallic Wars* could wait till we had mastered Latin's multiple inflections and intricate network of verbs. Religion was confined to the Ten Commandments and seven sacraments in the format of question and answer. We memorized verbatim without improvisation. Each morning after prayers and announcements, we heard: "Take out a half sheet of paper." A Latin quiz invariably followed one in Religion.

Jim was a pleasure to see. Older than the other scholastics, he was in his thirties, having been wounded during WW II for which he received a combat action badge, the Purple Heart. He was boyish in appearance with light brown hair parted high on his head, disarming blue eyes and a winsome smile that inched up the side of his face. Even when angry he smiled; the only sign of displeasure was the flush in his face and the gravity of his reply. His handsomeness was balanced by a dreamy, contemplative gaze. In conversation he would sometimes tilt his head to the side, look off in the distance, and pause as if hearing voices. His own was soft-spoken, his words unhurried. As he framed his thoughts, sincerity became their authority. When speaking, he moistened his lips to ease the chapping. A dry scalp produced flakiness on his black habit, and though it shocked me to see perfection compromised by dandruff, it humanized him.

When he leaned against the blackboard with one hand behind holding chalk, he doodled unconsciously. As he stepped away, we puzzled at his blackboard scribbling. It so resembled Chinese that Jim was also called Mr. Han Lee. He walked with a limp—the result of his war wound—and his slender frame barely held his cincture, which slipped to his thigh where it remained precariously.

His way of ranking Latin exams was distinctive. Classroom aisles were named after city streets: Fifth, Park, Flatbush, Bowery, and Skid Row. The last desk was 10 Skid Row; it became your address if the grade on your Latin exam was the worst in the class. You kept it till a stronger grade moved you to a more prestigious avenue. Every week we changed desks and addresses. Park Avenue might be exchanged for the Bowery because of a bad performance. The premier address was 1 Fifth which entitled its tenant, sitting front row front desk, to the name of Beetle. I competed for that premier piece of real estate with another boy, Salvatore Romano, who was equally adept at Latin. He and I alternated occupancy.

We were all sexually curious but shy; however, one precocious boy in the class, Peter Gambino, was blunt in asking about kissing and arousal. In these open sessions Hanley tolerated every question, even when the wording was crude.

"Sex looms high when you're young," he said, preferring a generalization to concrete details. "As you get older," he continued, "it takes its place among other ways of relating. You're young, and at your age it features strongly. It's only natural."

We wondered about his sexual life during the war, but only once did he advert to it:

"Soldiers coming to port were urged to be *continent*." The adjective puzzled us. He meant refraining from sexual relations while we saw a large land division on the planet.

The result of an anonymous question I submitted prompted Hanley's irritation. I asked about the *Kinsey Report* which was all the rage. He found my inquiry too current to be sincere. He dismissed it but did not ask anyone to acknowledge it.

I recall an outing to Radio City Music Hall. After the movie, we stopped in a store whose inventory of books was on sale. I was attracted to one, a technical study on musicology. The original price was steep, but it was marked down to a pittance. After I bought it, he asked:

"Does the subject interest you or does the reduced price?" He had exposed my shallowness. I never forgot the message: interest first, price later; it's a norm to which I still adhere in any purchase.

Jim was a person whose piety and wisdom united in an astutely Jesuit manner. I awaited his weekly criticism of my essays. He corrected in pencil and his penmanship was notable for its generous loops. He once commented on his religious vocation by writing in the margin: *"ad altiora natus sum"* (I was born for higher things). After a year of Latin I deciphered the words and grappled with their meaning. On another essay about feminine vanity, he remarked: "All right for the well-groomed woman who knows how to use cosmetics, but when the average high school girl is let loose with lipstick and a powder puff, the result is a candidate for any of our local menageries."

I did not know at the time he considered me a suitable candidate for the Society of Jesus. In my mother's diary I read how he had told her on parents' night: "Your son would make a good Jesuit." I had no interest in joining a religious order. I wanted to hang my mental gallery with strong male icons against which to compare myself. Jim's was the most prominent on my wall.

What I value most was our time together when the school day ended. He stopped me in the corridor to say he would be free later on, and could we meet in such and such a classroom. As a sophomore, I no longer called him my homeroom teacher, but he still showed interest by suggesting books for my reading: Alan Paton's *Too Late, the Phalarope* and *Cry, the Beloved Country*; Raïssa Maritain's memoirs, *We Have Been Friends Together* and *Adventures in Grace*; Charles Péguy's *Basic Verities*, and Léon Bloy's *Pilgrim of the Absolute*. I have since reread them all, and they still enrich with their humane insight into truth.

When I arrived from school in time for dinner, my father noticed the late hour and asked where I'd been: "Talking to Mr. Hanley," I said, repeating the words every time. I think he envied Jim's influence, which far exceeded his own. I was captivated for I could not learn enough about this man. I listened with rapt attention to his stories of the trenches, his wound and convalescence, and his reflections on career after surviving the war. Years later when I read Somerset Maugham's *The Razor's Edge*, the character of Larry Darrell, a survivor of war, so reminded me of Jim that they mentally merged. Perhaps that's why I recommend the novel: to keep Jim's memory alive.

By the time I entered junior year Mr. Hanley had left to study theology. He was ordained a priest in his third year, but I did not attend; I was ensconced in a Jesuit novitiate near the Canadian border, rarely traveling farther than the main road. I saw him once during my philosophical studies. He had put on weight and was no longer the slim-hipped scholastic. Still, he managed to remain boyish. We picnicked on the seminary grounds, and I was pleased at the appetite with which he ate the lunch I had packed. But I was less successful with the dessert. While I enjoyed the oatmeal cookies, they proved inedible to him. "I dislike raisins," he said. He voiced his preference in the Hanley manner: firmly but with no desire to offend. It was another lesson in candor.

Years later, as a teacher at Brooklyn Prep, I learned Father Hanley had left the priesthood. Once laicized, he married a woman he knew during the war. I think she was Belgian and may have been his nurse. He phoned me at school one day and asked to see me. He was coming up from Washington where he held an administrative post in a hospital. We met in Grand Central Station, then took the train to the village where we lunched at an outdoor café. I recall no details of the conversation but only his efforts to explain his leaving the priesthood. He felt he owed me an explanation since his mentoring had influenced my religious vocation. His decision did not pain me, for I had passed on to other mentors. That visit shaped another maxim: each of us is irreplaceable but eminently substitutable. We gratefully remember our forebears but press on.

To this day I retain Jim's address and phone number, though I've never communicated with him. Without corroboration I believe he thinks of me; that he recalls with pleasure the friendship between a boy of fifteen and a man in his thirties.

After Jim left prep other Jesuits filled the gap: there was John Culkin who was six foot four with a broad physique and a receding hairline that resembled a runway of brown stubble. A man of unruffled confidence, he appeared arrogant; on closer inspection, he geared his shrewd mind to a student's best interests. And he did this with the jocks, aesthetes, and intellectuals. He regularly exchanged his black habit for athletic shorts and appeared on the gym floor. His hoop shot could sink a basketball as easily as he could collapse an opponent trying to hack him. Formidable under any circumstance, whether dribbling down the court or clinching an argument, he was athlete, classicist, and humanist all at once, a man of such wide appeal he held us in considerable awe. Another type in the cast of Jesuit characters, he was the mentor whose aggressive manner had the lilt of refinement.

He spoke like a TV journalist, his sentences clipped like sound bites, and he nodded his head to confirm their invincible truth. Often his words had a note of irony. Whenever they were sarcastic, you tolerated them, however stinging, for fear you might invite a sharper barb. He was the counselor whose pragmatism had the ring of revelation. If you tried supplementing his view, his reply suggested your insight was implied in his own. It was best to play disciple. The fixity of his gaze could be unnerving, for he never blinked as he rendered judgment. Rome had spoken when Jack had.

I remember once how he asked the class to translate a tedious section of Xenophon's *Anabasis*. It was dull going: raw statistics about how many parasangs the foot soldiers had traveled. The assignment was to render the Greek in prose reflecting the original. Instead of imitating Xenophon's flat style, I translated with verve unwarranted by the text. My embellished version pleased me, for it was what I thought Xenophon should have written. The next day my paper was returned awash in red ink. I recall the acid delivery of Jack's comment; it flashed like a neon sign: "Too much Rocco, not enough Zeno." His criticism taught me what I recognized years later: exuberance joined to willfulness makes me do it my way. That instinct, harnessed correctly, has been the source of a lively imagination, for I recast what's there in my image and likeness. But the tendency has the defects of the quality: it prefers inventiveness to strict truth for the sake of vivacity.

Jack was my junior year instructor in ancient Greek. Under his guidance, I began reading Homer's *Odyssey* and modern paperbacks—a new phenomenon in the fifties. I was thrilled with my copy of *The Sayings of the Compassionate Buddha*; even then I evinced an interest in Asian thought which Jack encouraged. Because of him, I was put into a program for the school's brightest boys, who became known as Super Greeks. Everything—from science and mathematics to classical language and modern literature—was at a college level. The *hoi polloi* might have thought us eggheads had it not been for several athletes who democratized the class.

Jack was ordained a Jesuit priest but later left the ministry. I was not surprised for I could never see him in a liturgical role. His humanism transcended the constraints of all religions, which functioned for him like instruments in an orchestra where he alone was maestro.

I recall Fr. Robert Haskins, the student counselor, conspicuous for his sunglasses, cigarettes, and Jesuit cape worn over his habit. He made you feel special as he drew you into his confidence. "This is *entre nous*," he said, using the French phrase that conveys privacy. I soon learned that what he had confided was "between us" and the whole school. From Haskins came my taste for sunglasses—I own several—and a preference for things European.

Haskins felt responsible for the football players who might otherwise have been missed. Whether massively built or wiry, he called them "small boys," and they were attracted to his swagger, metallic laughter, and dashing good looks. The honor students who eschewed athletics judged him harshly, calling him (behind his back) not Fr. Haskins but Father Asskiss; they decided he bent too far over to attract the jocks. He seemed intent on avoiding boys in the top tier, having left them to the savoir faire of other Jesuits who won their allegiance.

I remember Father Andrew Brady, master of novices, and head of the Jesuit novitiate: jowly, steely in character, moving unimpeded with the intrepid velocity of an armored car. His blue eyes were so penetrating they lasered at a glance. He taught and terrified me into the rudiments of Jesuit life. I still hear him instructing us at the novices' morning conference:

"Ours must avoid singularity. SJ after your names is remarkable enough. You must never cultivate oddity to draw attention. You're part of the Long Black Line stretching back to our founder, St. Ignatius, and disappearing into the horizon." To dramatize his point he pounded his fist on the conference table: "Nothing singular, I tell you and nothing lah-de-dah. Oddity in behavior must be eschewed at all costs." Brady had favorite verbs and adjectives which he repeated with regularity. For "avoid" he said "eschew"; for "childish" he said "jejune"; they were meant to dispel apathy in the practice of Jesuit spirituality:

"Beloved in Christ," he continued, "each of you is to be *'instrumentum conjunctum Deo'* [an instrument joined to God] so that all your actions, raised to a supernatural level, are used for God's greater glory.

"You are companions of Jesus similar to the way a man is companion to his wife. His love for her permeates the day without having to think about it. It's like background music. From time to time a man stops and listens to reanimate his work. The love is always there to contemplate and enjoy. You too must be contemplative *'sive in actione sive in oratione'* [whether in action or in prayer]. It's the special charism of St. Ignatius passed on to his sons: the love of God spilling into service. Nothing must impede it. But if ever you find the need for human intimacy that great, just admit it and get out." Never mincing his words, he was blunt in his demands.

I think Brady recognized my literary ability and saw me as a natural contemplative. In his gruff manner he encouraged my talent for poetry. He was drawn to those novices whom he viewed as "artistes"—another of his words—but his attraction was tinged with suspicion. He kept alert for signs that the artistic impulse had slipped into oddity. I cite one incident which confirmed in his mind that I had acted "singularly." It was the Jesuit version of Big Brother Is Looking at You. Recalling the event makes me shudder.

Every six months Brady chose a set of house officials for the novitiate. His secretary was called the manuductor, and he was assigned the task of setting the strict daily order and any exceptions to it. Other house titles indicated their jurisdiction: guest master, grounds, and choir. I was put in charge of the dining room, in Latin *triclinium*, with the eponymous title of *triclinarius*. Since Bellarmine College had once been a prestige resort on Lake Champlain, I had inherited a stock of silver and dinnerware worthy of a turn-of-the-century watering hole. But breakage was inevitable when trying to accommodate over two hundred people. After taking inventory one morning, I realized we were running short of bread plates; there were not enough to complete the individual place settings. I brought my problem to Father George Murphy, Socius to the master of novices, and responsible for handling material needs. He thanked me for keeping him apprised:

"I'll order bread plates immediately. I doubt they'll be perfectly matched so there's no use in trying. If I can order plastic, I'll do so. It will avoid a future problem."

The bread plates arrived in a week's time, and I had my novice team distribute them after dinner one night so they were ready for breakfast the next morning. They were plastic as promised, but they were also a startling grass green. With white dishes and tablecloths, the color jumped from the plates. Green had shattered the white uniformity. The next morning after community Mass, I headed for the dining room and checked to see that the bread plates were in place. I then sat at first table where I had an early breakfast. Again I looked around to see that the plates were properly aligned on the Fathers' tables facing my own. Father Murphy had ordered correctly; plastic rendered them unbreakable.

Breakfast that morning proved to be a favorite: scrambled eggs and bacon; steaming cornbread with maple syrup and butter. As I started to eat,

I glanced over to check if the priests had been served. I noted the master of novices in his place, but his face seemed hardened in an expression of acute displeasure. His eyes were glaring in my direction, his pupils dilated like a cat's accommodating the darkness. His glance at me was not at eye level but came from the lowered angle of one looking up as if full view was intolerable. Something was amiss, indeed deeply and irretrievably wrong; something in which I was implicated but could not say what. Appetite for the food on my plate dissipated with my growing alarm. I rose without finishing, said my thanksgiving prayer, left my plate on the mobile cart, and moved to the chapel for the required visit. As I genuflected and exited from the entrance, my eyes lowered in the gesture of modesty, I heard someone sidling up and felt a tap on my shoulder. It was Brady. His face was flushed with rage.

"Hey, boy," he said. It was a salutation he used when his anger was scarcely in check. I have heard that direct address, "boy," used only of Negroes on southern plantations where the white overseers employed it to belittle grown men. Something in my actions triggered the same disrespect. I felt the blood leave my face and my hands grow cold as my stomach growled involuntarily.

"Yes, Father," I said, and then awaited the inevitable.

With a swift movement of his right hand, he reached into the voluminous pocket of his Jesuit habit and pulled out a green bread plate.

"What's the meaning of this?" he asked as he held it in front of me like a huge green communion wafer. I was so nonplussed I began to stutter. I did not grasp the intent of his question.

"Did you hear me, boy?" he repeated.

"Yes, Father."

"What does this mean?" he said explosively.

"It's a bread plate," I replied.

"I know what it is. Do you think I'm blind? Who gave you permission to put this out?"

Suddenly I caught the gist of his anger. He had assumed that the green bread plate was an act of independent judgment; more egregiously, I had foisted my peculiar choice on the whole community who now had to live with it. I had acted singularly. Here was proof positive that my temperament—the "artiste" in me—had run amok. He had inveighed against the impulse in conference, and I was boldly and impudently testing his counsel. My action needed to be rebuffed, the perversity in my nature expunged. Otherwise, some new deviancy might be waiting in the wings.

"Well?" Brady asked, his voice modulating, "What have you to say?"

"Father Master, it was Father Murphy who ordered the bread plates and then asked me to put them out. We didn't have enough of the white ones to go around."

Suddenly Brady realized his error and how colossally he had misjudged the situation. Without any apology for misreading my motives, he took the bread plate, pressed it between my hands, and left me in the middle of the foyer slightly spastic while holding the green plastic.

When after two years I had completed my Jesuit novitiate, Brady approved me for first vows but not without warning me during the final interview. I do not know if residues of the green bread plate colored his parting words:

"You're an artiste. You have to watch that. You're also sensate. You have to watch that too." On both accounts he proved right. He was a gemologist who cut and polished; or to put it more classically, he was a mentor who imprinted himself on those who later became imprinters, all raising up human memorials "more lasting than bronze."

The Jesuit priest who made an enduring impact on my life was Fr. Daniel Berrigan. What better way to respond to my fifty-five-year-old friendship with him than to cite an aphorism of Cardinal Avery Dulles, who, in commenting on doctrinal development has insisted that if it is genuine it is true to its roots: "Origins are given once and for all," he writes with quotability. In the light of that judgment, I return to a March day in 1955 when Dan and I first met. I do it with the composition of place made so real by an application of the senses, that I summon up the memory and enliven the cliché, "It seems like yesterday."

As a member of the sophomore Sodality of the Blessed Virgin, I found myself in Father Berrigan's company taking a Brooklyn bus to the Gold Street Mission. Dan had been asked to substitute for the moderator, who was tutoring students in the lower mysteries of plane geometry. I knew Dan by sight as the priest with the abstracted air who did not so much traverse school corridors as waft through them. He had not yet won the Lamont prize for *Time Without Number*, but his repute as a poet preceded him. His preaching at the first Friday Mass was my exposure to his beguiling way with words. I recall one sermon in which he warned the students against "the illusion of the obvious." Opaque to me then, this phrase has since become demonstrably clear. On that March day, as I sat beside him in awe of the poet, I recall how he put me at ease, and how swiftly we seemed to arrive at our destination.

Dan and I walked to the mission and entered a ramshackle building where the security guard directed us to the auditorium. Chairs in clusters encircled the room in which Catholic students were catechizing their charges. Dan left to explore the premises while I joined my Communion class. Five students from the previous week were dutifully waiting, but I noted a sixth had been added—Winston. Five feet tall and wiry, he was dressed in the oversized clothes of an older brother. Dark complexioned with huge eyes and coal black irises, he did not so much sit in his chair as squirm in it. He muttered aloud as his eyes looked distractedly ahead. Here was a needy child.

I hoped to explain how Catholic Mass incorporated the Jewish Passover. I never got that far. Winston twisted and turned, waving both hands, or interrupted with pointless remarks. When to the cheers of the class he landed on the floor with his collapsible chair alongside, I lost my patience. I did not notice Dan watching from a distance. He walked over and without explaining asked Winston: "Would you like a soda?" He nodded yes, eager to exchange my presence for a newcomer's. Order returned and my class moved peaceably to its close. I glanced across the room to see Winston sipping his soda. Dan sat alongside with a smile compounded of kindness and genial irony. I gave my students their assignment and dismissed them, then walked over to Winston who was slurping the remainder of his coke. Without soda to distract, I thought, who will calm his antics, for he had now inserted a finger in the neck of the soda bottle, and was banging it against the chair. Dan turned to him.

"Winston, would you like to hear a story?"

"What story?" he asked.

"About the genie in the Coca Cola bottle."

"What's a genie?"

I excused myself and walked away, having decided that the improvised tale was between Dan and Winston. I regret not staying for the story of a spirit, locked in a bottle, but eager for freedom to benefit the conjurer. At five o'clock the security guard sounded the bell that signaled the building's close. I saw Dan holding Winston's hand as they approached his mother waiting at the door.

"Were you good today, Winston?" she asked.

He nodded affirmatively while Dan smiled in confirmation. Winston waved good-bye as we left the building, and then Dan and I returned to Brooklyn Prep. I remember nothing of our conversation on the bus, nor do I recall being in his presence again, for shortly after he left to teach theology. In later years we met in Jesuit houses: Bellarmine College, Loyola

Seminary, and Woodstock College, frequently when I came down from Harvard, more often when I resided in New York. But the value of that first encounter stayed with me as a symbol of Dan's life and of what was to come. For I have been privy to his multiple incarnations: priest, poet, theologian, playwright, peacemaker, consoler of the sick and dying—the names on the brass plate seem legion. His genie, that Berrigan élan bottled up first in Danbury prison and then later in countless jails, has been summoned, time without number, out of compassion for many.

In my own life, I have domiciled in palaces and hovels; have frequented the gold coast of Italy and the slums of Bangkok. All of it is grist for the writer's imagination. But I can think of nothing more engaging than to sit in a café with Dan sipping a cappuccino: a latter-day Winston engrossed in an episode of the saga called Dan's life. The tension mitigates as the lilt of his voice confirms that all will be well. I leave him reinstated, reassured, revived. Origins are indeed given *once and for all*, but then the best things are: poetry and prayer, music and friendship, and Daniel. "Once and for all"—how solid a statement this is in our mutable world. No illusion, and not for one moment obvious.

So here they are, five mentors from my youth: a visionary, a humanist, a dandy, a martinet, and a prophet. What one can surmise is that the Jesuits were dominant in my youth and thereafter. In a novel, *Fire in a Windless Place*, I acknowledged their influence through the main character, Dr. David McCauley. His contact with them is recalled with grudging praise:

> The Jesuits, when I first met them, were the most glamorous order in the church, stars in an otherwise drab, ecclesiastical sky. Their cultural attainments, encompassing a humane theology, were a blend of missionary zeal and worldliness. They seemed forever on the verge of tottering, their tightrope strung between opposing poles with no net below to break the fall.

One gasped at the high jinks as they kept their difficult balance between binary forces: individualism and blind obedience; maverick intellectuality and church loyalty; sensuality and unwavering celibacy. But one questioned the sanity of feats demonstrated at such precarious heights, weighed down as the Jesuits were with such ambivalence.

To the doctor's credit, toward the novel's end he develops a more generous attitude, and so did I. A poem in limericks written years later confirms my gratitude:

St. Ignatius and the Jesuits

In an age overtly rapacious,
Where newspaper ads are salacious,
And pride, lust, and greed
Prompt thought, word, and deed—
How refreshing to read St. Ignatius.

His prayer, "Lord, take and receive,"
Makes the covetous stand up and leave.
To risk it and stay
Is to be in harm's way—
Better go fast than chance to believe.

Not so the Jesuit priest:
He's steadfast, to say the least:
A touch eremitical
And equally critical
Of angel, God, man, or beast.

What lies at the Jesuit's core
Is the restless idea of "the more";
From his spiritual garrison
Of Gospel comparison,
Nothing ever stays as before.

So "Jesuit" means having nerve
To stand up and offer to serve.
Despite jail or censure,
The Christian adventure
Accounts for the vigor and verve.

If you're looking for quick-acting balm
Or the joys of a bucolic psalm,
It's galloping turtles
Or squaring of circles
To speak of a Jesuit: calm.

His calling's to do it or die,
The cost is me, self, and I.
If you want the amenity
Of constant serenity,
It's elsewhere you'd better apply.

No Jesuit claps hands or sings
Of the source from which all of this springs.
You may disapprove
Of his prayer on the move:
He's just finding God in all things.

So the heart of the Jesuit's call
Is like that of saints Peter and Paul.
The dangerous fact
Is the balancing act
Of no net to cushion the fall.

In an age overtly voracious,
Where theater and films are fallacious,
And envy and rage
Are presented as sage,
How bracing the task
To speak of this Basque:
In mind so vivacious,
In heart so capacious:
What a godsend to have St. Ignatius.

I can hear my imaginary reader saying: "Fine about the Jesuits. But I want to hear about your companions. Who were they, and what happened to them?"

To answer you, I will start with my high school friends. We moved in an all-male group because Brooklyn Prep was an all-boys school. The local girls' school was there for socials, but friends came from prep. One Jesuit scholastic, George Driscoll, called us "culture vultures." It was an apt description. Apart from extracurriculars like the drama club, newspaper, or school magazine, we enjoyed classical music, foreign films, museums, and exchanging books. Outside prep, our dealings with one another centered on the late night party we called the soirée. We took turns arranging for it, and it lasted well past midnight to the chagrin of our parents who listened for the key in the door. Food, drink, dessert, and coffee were always served. Mandatory too were insults exposing illegitimacy.

The faces remain clear after decades. I will use first names and initialed surnames to individuate:

A lifelong friend and my best antidote to hokum, was Joe L., whose agnosticism had more in common with Thomas Aquinas than Bertrand Russell. His acute reasoning dissipated in a cloud of incense whenever he celebrated Russian liturgy. In the course of doctoral work, I was reminded of him during Buddhist lectures. I learned how Nagarjuna, an Indian pundit, wielded logic like a machete. Joe's logic, too, reduced inflexible doctrine to nonsense. Since to go beyond sense was a trait of the sacred, he pressed his negation into the service of piety. His mysticism had less to do with schism than the dispersal of mist: that opaque language presuming to know God from the inside. Joe was likely to quip: "God is invisible, intangible, indescribable, and ineffable—all the qualities of nothing at all." Your faith might run scared from the assault of his reasoning unless you acknowledged that all religious language was provisional; that you'd bolster your faith less with creeds than with billowing smoke and bursts of Slavonic chant.

My best memories are the evenings at his home listening to classical music. He introduced me to Tchaikovsky, and we heard the Pathétique and 1812 Overture countless times. Exchanging books became a ritual: my copy of Malraux's *Man's Fate* for his of McCullers, *The Heart is a Lonely Hunter*. At his suggestion, I first read *Brideshead Revisited* on the Toms River, and then *Look Homeward, Angel*. I seemed always to have a novel Joe had passed on to elicit my judgment. The informal book club continued even during my graduate studies when he introduced me to Iris Murdoch whose novels have proved a constant delight.

I remember Joe P. whose rich tenor voice made him an asset in any musical comedy. He was short, about five foot four, rotund rather than fat, with a laugh like a Gatling gun that abated to giggles. As a low-life character, he was a must in any Shakespearean comedy. Prancing derisively, he pretended sexual ardor for one or another of us by sidling up, rolling his eyes, and shivering as if he had been furtively fondled. We convulsed with laughter at his rendition of the martyrdom of St. Agnes, whose virginity was threatened because she refused a centurion's advances. Joe played the Roman as an effeminate soldier whose soprano lisp, "Yeth, yeth!" contrasted with Agnes's basso, "No, no!" The shifts in pitch were rapid, the role reversal quick. A robust Agnes, feigning resistance, finally yields to the puny Roman with an orgasmic cry, "O brother!"

Juvenile antics shaped our dealings with one another like the drama staged on a train station. We called it *The Humming Homo*. Joe P. and another friend, Chris L., hummed loudly at opposite ends of the platform; then rushing with open arms toward each other like separated lovers missed by running past. More fatuous still was our treatment of Ruth Hussey, an actress from the fifties. Her last name was the object of sarcasm. She had played the Virgin Mary in a mawkish nativity film in which she called her husband, Joe-zef. When anyone of us called Joseph was addressed, the reply was always, "Yes, Ruth."

The soirées we enjoyed went from buffet eating to exclusive drinking, and left us in an alcoholic haze. We were learning to hold our wine and not to mix drinks disastrously. Tipsy by the evening's end, we managed sobriety to share in the harmonies of "Evaline," "Moonlight Bay," and "In the Still of the Night," all from our glee club repertoire.

Some of our best parties were at Ken H's. My exits from his house at three in the morning put me at odds with my parents, who lay awake until I returned. Ken's mother was the subject of genial humor. With a whisky sour in one hand, she seemed permanently dressed for a gala. The hat she never removed was sometimes flower-rimmed, sometimes tiered. I saw her without it once and realized her hair was thinning. She hid her condition by stylish hats bought from the local milliner's. At two in the morning she served brewed coffee with light cream together with pastries. Her son, Ken, played host. He had milky skin, colorless hair, and deep blue eyes. His albino condition accounted for the thick glasses. He removed them occasionally and pressed the print to his eyes for easier access. Ken became a Benedictine monk in Benet Lake, Wisconsin. He had a beautiful tenor voice suited for navigating the rise and fall of Gregorian. In a mocking mood he broke into chant whose improvised words were a string of double entendres. His was the first religious vocation sprung from our group. I count six to the priesthood and as many to religious life. These were pursued with fitful success, for several ended in marginal compliance or late departure. How do I account for the number? Was it the homoerotic air like sweet-smelling gas that hung over everything? My friends and I dated vigorously, but girls were for dances, socials, and proms. Heterosexual intensity when it did occur was confined to romantic friendships. I had several but one stands out for its unhappy timing.

Shortly after applying to the Jesuits and being accepted, I met Lucille French. I have celebrated that meeting in a novel called *Portrait of a Woman* in which a young novelist, Philip Stratton, is smitten with an older woman in his imagination, and then constructs what it would have been like to love her as a contemporary. In the novel within the novel, I used my Sunday meeting with Lucille in Sheepshead Bay, Brooklyn, when she walked to St. Mark's Church for Mass. I transposed the event to Cambridge, Massachusetts, where the young woman Philip follows is called Bliss and later Daria when he learns her real name.

The lyrical description of Daria is drawn from my first visual impression of Lucille, whose auburn hair was swept up in a French twist. I cite from the novel: "Her face haunts me: the dark eyes, her skin the color of apple blossom, the forehead and arched brows, the cheekbones and shapely mouth. She had stepped from a fresco."

I dated Lucille for six months prior to entering the Jesuits on July 30, 1958. During that time, I seem to have forgotten my impending date of entrance. I escorted her to prep's dances and to dinner at the Tavern on the Green. She was an excellent dresser, and her choice in clothes—I recall a multicolored bubble dress—was enhanced by superb carriage and a graceful walk. She seemed intensely to inhabit her body as she communed with her own thoughts, and her contemplative air lent an aura of mystery.

I have found a photo of the two of us in my parents' living room. I am sitting on the piano bench with a cigarette in hand—a Turkish Oval—while she sits alongside adjusting my French beret which has slipped to the side. After that visit, she sent me a Valentine's Day card addressed: *"Pour Joe,"* and signing it *"Avec tout mon amour, The Contessa."* More accurately, she was a baroness. The coat of arms prominently displayed on her living room wall belonged to the Barons de Freyne, descendants of Arthur French, the first baron. His title in the peerage of the United Kingdom was created in 1851; his ancestral seat was the French Park Estate near County Roscommon in the Republic of Ireland. Their manor house built in the 1600s was demolished in 1952 after the French family sold the estate to the Irish Land Commission.

Lucille's family descended from the seventh Baron de Freyne who died in 2009, but I don't know the details of her lineage. The current heir apparent, Alexander French, is Lucille's distant relative. Her mother's forebears were Italian, and while I knew her grandmother hailed from Italy, I never learned her marriage name. Lucille had an unidentical twin sister, Loretta, who was quite charming, but Lucille was the great beauty with the demeanor of a born *contessa*. It was thus that I introduced her to my friends at prep who teased me—to my satisfaction—about dating a peer of the realm. Lucille married a cousin of my classmate, Henry Cavanna, and my mother and father attended the ceremony. I have a photo of bride and bridegroom flanked by their families and my parents. In her wedding gown Lucille looks radiant, for she was at the apex of her loveliness.

During my first year as a Jesuit novice, I had my manifestation of conscience with Father Brady. I was frank in revealing that Lucille had filled my mind with multiple images none of which inclined toward chastity.

"You have a week to decide," he said bluntly. "It's either us or her."

I chose the Jesuits.

Lucille lives on in *Portrait of a Woman* in the person of Daria. Whenever I revisit those pages in which Philip follows her to church, loses her in the crowd, and embodies his grief in poetry, I'm brought back in memory to that first love which eluded me then but which, through the conjuring power of fiction, remains with me still.

For all the late adolescent infatuation, no one of my friends ever "hooked up" in our current parlance. Premarital sex and cohabitation were forbidden because of our connection to the church. The only women in proximity were our mothers who dominated the scene. We were all in turn intensely devout and largely male-exclusive, for our sexuality was on hold. Testosterone levels, described as raging hormones, were kept under wraps by the example of the Jesuits. Their celibate presence proved victorious.

In my coterie of chums the zest for friendship has its origin; I paid tribute to it in *Fire in a Windless Place* through the ruminations of the main character, David McCauley:

> Friendship, what is summed up in that word? What nobility
> of mind and heart, indifferent to all but character, resides in

those two syllables? Despite its abdication to romantic love by some mistaken right of succession, with stubborn loyalty we cling to it still as heir to the throne of our affections, and in our dotage we continue to pay it homage. What mysterious bonding at the outset accounts for friendship? Is it some rush of recognition given in a phrase or gesture, or is it conferred by a glance that allows a glimpse of the complete soul? Whatever the origins, we delight in the riches dispensed over a lifetime: the companionable silences that never embarrass; the admonitions born of esteem; the disinterested caring that hides no agenda. It is wholly communion, two composing a solitude, warmth from a mutual fire.

vi

I had just returned to New York City from a trip to Sicily where I toured archeological sites on both coasts. What brought me to the land of my paternal grandparents was a meeting the prior summer while staying at the Casa Internazionale. A palazzo on the Via della Scrofa, it houses priests on a daily or monthly basis. The casa is a papal enclave outside Italian jurisdiction. Since I planned to be in Rome for a friend's graduation, the residence seemed congenial for its location near the Piazza Navona and its modest per diem, a pittance in contrast to the tariffs of the local hotels. Three meals and a quiet room with private bath for seventy euros was a pontifical bargain.

When I checked in at the casa and waited for my assigned room, I noticed how the desk clerk Massimo studied my information form. I sat waiting until he called my name, "Padre Giuseppe." I walked over and he handed me my key saying, "I think you will like the room. If anything further is needed, please call on me." I thanked him and took the lift to the third floor. The room was easily reached, for it was central on the main landing.

When I entered and saw the amenities, I was astonished: a bedroom and large bath; a sitting room with desk, easy chair, and library alcove—it was more a suite for a prelate than an American priest on holiday. I was sure it was a mistake. There was no way that seventy euros earned such generous accommodations. I took the stairs in twos and found myself alone with the desk clerk. We conducted our conversation in Italian, which I'll render in English:

"Massimo," I said, "I think you've made an error and given me the key to the wrong room." He looked at the key and number.

"The room is correct, Padre Giuseppe. Don't you like it?"

"Of course I like it. It's spacious and quiet. But it seems more fitting for a bishop or dignitary. I'm neither."

"But your last name is special. It has a long lineage. Didn't you know?"

I wanted to wave my right hand over my shoulder in the way Italians do when they've seen through an exaggeration and reply, "Ma quando? Mai," the gesture meaning, "But when? Never." I was too respectful of Massimo to question his sincerity.

"Your name is noble," he said, "and I respect it. The surnames, Rocca and Salvo, have been joined to form one word. But if you visit the Libreria Borghese on the Via dei Trotti, you will find the *Golden Book of Italian Nobility*. The second volume gives the history of your families dating back to the thirteenth century before they intermarried. Italy may be a republic, but we respect our forebears. Yours are illustrious. They include marquises and barons, feudal lords and bishops, and doctors of law and knights of Malta. The room I assigned you is a sign of my respect."

I now have the two volumes on my bookshelf, and I have examined the requisite pages. Massimo's remarks were accurate. Since that meeting, I have used the accompanying shields (*gli stemmi*) of the Roccas and the Salvos for my business card. I had it embossed, so that a person receiving it would retain the card for its aesthetic merit. On each heraldic shield is a cross: on the Rocca shield it's at the summit of three peaks; on the Salvo shield it's in the talons of a rampant lion with a rising seven-pointed star.

Blue, red, and gold comprise the palette of colors while the Latin motto, "In Deo Salus," (In God Salvation) expresses the family motto.

I do not think Grandma and Grandpa Roccasalvo had any awareness of ancestral nobility. They were humbly born in the province of Ragusa, in the southeastern city of Vittoria; it has since become a prosperous provincial town, among the wealthiest, in Sicily. Farming of fertile grounds, modern cultivation, and an outstanding agricultural market have created the wealth. But such conditions did not prevail during my grandparents' youth. First cousins on their maternal side, they received a dispensation to marry. Shortly after, in their twenties, they took the boat to America, proceeding first to Ellis Island where a record of their arrival in 1901 is extant.

My grandparents lived on the lower East Side where my father's grandparents later joined them in 1913. A gas leak caused their tragic deaths. Perhaps it was my father who found them dead. All his life he dealt with a compulsion "to check the gas jets." Often returning after we had left the apartment to reexamine the stove, he studied the knobs to confirm they were in the off position. Unhappily he passed on this habit to me, and I have to resist the impulse to repeat the neurotic ritual.

My father was born in 1906 and died shortly before his seventieth birthday in 1976. As a young man he went to public school but completed his college curriculum in 1928 at the private Beverly Academy in Brooklyn. He educated his gifted hands—for his touch was poignant and powerful—by studying medical massage at the Swedish Institute; later he rehabilitated hundreds of patients with debilities from polio, Parkinson's disease, muscular dystrophy, and stroke. After hours of Greek and Latin translation, with my head on the verge of a migraine, I went to my father for help. By the quick adjustment of my neck and spine, he neutralized the throbbing pain and I returned to my homework, refreshed.

Grandpa Roccasalvo went from bricklayer to working for New York's Department of Transportation. His shrewd management of money enabled him to buy real estate, and he was the proud owner of two houses around the corner from each other. I resided most of my childhood at 1311 Avenue Z, a one family walk-up; the house is still there and displays the same sphere of glass on the front door above the numerical address. Grandpa's industry was not confined to salaried work. At home on Twelfth Street, he planted a garden where he grew tomatoes, green and yellow squash, purple eggplant, fragrant basil, and enormous concord grapes. His tomato sauce, homemade wine, and liqueurs were enviable, and he was the one who taught Grandma to cook. But he remained master chef. I can still smell the wine bubbling in casks, the liqueur redolent of anise, the orange rind in curls giving off their resinous crackle before the stove as they scented the basement. My dealings with him involved the foods he prepared for saints' days like St. Joseph and major feasts like Christmas and Easter. I watched him meticulously chop and mix ingredients.

After my brother and I were born, he held us in his two arms like trophies; we were the heirs apparent to the Roccasalvo name. But when, one by one, his grandchildren were drawn to religious life, his Sicilian anticlericalism made him recoil in anger:

"Why does my son allow this?" he scowled. "Is he running a church?"

And when before I left for the Jesuits, I visited him to say good-bye; he reached into his pocket and gave me a hundred dollar bill with the caustic remark:

"*Buona fortuna, vostro Eminenza*" ("Good luck, your Eminence"). I tried to hug him but he pushed me away.

When the Dominican Sisters at St. Rose's Home later cared for him as he suffered from terminal cancer, he softened his resolve. From the

Jesuit novitiate I wrote him a letter in Italian, not knowing how to pen my thoughts in Sicilian. He never replied, but my mother told me he received it well. When he died on April 9, 1960, I was still in religious formation and not permitted to attend his funeral. Had he been my mother or father, protocol would have been different. Although he helped to raise me as an infant, that early intervention did not ease canonical constraints. I remember my grief at being absent, but such were the rigors of a pre-Vatican II church.

Attentive, loving, and always carrying me when Pina was not there, Grandma Roccasalvo in contrast to Grandpa was temperamentally bland. She kept her own counsel and usually bowed to his patriarchal demands; however, it was she who arranged for my temporary adoption, and her intransigence at surrendering me early rescued my mother from a nervous breakdown. My grandfather had a Vesuvial temper, and it was best not to be near when he spewed forth his anger. But he knew how to accede to my grandmother when she resolved an issue, and so agreed to my living with them. It was not until her death in 1952, eight years before his, that I realized how much he cherished her. He plaintively called out her name, "Peppina, Peppina," and we could do nothing to assuage his pain which inevitably hastened his death.

My trip to Sicily to discover my familial roots had a second purpose, for I was working on the dramatization of a short story, *The Siren*, by Giuseppe di Lampedusa. To learn more about the author, I visited his home in Palermo and country estate at Santa Margherita. I was eager to establish the story's composition of place, and my trips viewing temples and statuary enriched my imagination. When I finally returned to New York, I had a sheaf of notes and corroborative photos; they would prove invaluable in dramatizing Lampedusa's incomparable story. I felt rested and primed for writing, since the two hotels where I stayed had offered me five star comfort and companionship. My Sicilian holiday had bolstered my decision to stay put and write.

No sooner had I returned than I found a phone message from a professor of drama at NYU's Tisch School. He was a long-standing friend who dated back to our seminary days when we both had majored in classics. I was happy to hear his voice, and he matched my eagerness to catch up.

"Let's meet for lunch at Dean & Deluca. You can share travel anecdotes, and I'll pick up the tab. Now that you're back I have to tell you what happened. You'll never guess whose play I saw. It's too bad you didn't arrive earlier because it had a run of just two weeks. A fellow seminarian wrote it—a closer friend of yours than mine. You remember Nathan Darcie. Well, his play was brilliant. I'm not surprised. You recall his flair for poetry, how it competed with his course work. His talent has paid off. He received wonderful reviews. I have a playbill for you. It will give you some idea what Darcie's been up to."

In my diary I penciled in lunch the next day and confirmed it on Scott's answering service. If I hadn't been feeling acute jet lag, I would have left bags unpacked and met Scott immediately, so jolted was I by news of Nathan.

I had not heard his name for half a century, nor once ever seen it in print. But as soon as he was mentioned, Nathan's face invaded my mind and multiplied like shards of a broken mirror. His play's warm reception by New York critics came as a revelation. If I ever thought of him, it was never as a playwright but as our seminary's most gifted poet. He was several years my senior. Since I was new at writing poetry, I viewed him in seminary as my exemplar, for his mastery of rhythm and rhyme was dazzling. Content and verse form were so perfectly paired that every word fell artlessly in place. His poems, demanding to be read aloud, seemed meant for performance. It was here he discovered his passion for the theater.

I scoured an album of photos to find one of him in his twenties. It was a group picture taken before the doors of the Jesuit seminary. Dressed in black cassock like his classmates, he sat with hands decorously on his knees while a shy smile strained to be social. His face, notable for its good looks, high color, and deep set eyes reminded me of a painting by Modigliani. With a scissors I cut out his likeness to awaken my memory.

After five decades why was news about Nathan tugging at me? Was he a symbol of my seminary years? I wanted to pore over the past and remember every shared experience: the lakeside walks, the bantering words, the poetic sparring—each incident seemed vital in creating a complete picture. But what could I hope to rescue? Whoever we were no longer existed for our youth was gone. Still, something irrepressible rang in the corridor of memory. As heir of a former friendship, I had to know what made up its legacy. Buddhism told me nothing stayed the same, but it also warned me nothing was entirely different. Did anything remain of the friend I knew and would I recognize him? In an effort to answer this question, I take my cue from Waugh's *Brideshead Revisited*; I'm tempted to call this section of my memoir, "The Sacred and Profane Memories of Nathaniel Darcie," and to affirm like Waugh the selfsame purpose: "my theme is memory."

I see him in my mind's eye almost fifty years ago on a July day of brilliant sun and lakeside breezes. Cumulus clouds punctuated the sky while the scents of the ambient gardens were everywhere. Not a trace of humidity freighted the air—it was more like June than high summer—for it had poured torrentially the night before. Now everything: grass, foliage, lawns, and hedges were shades of neon green. The combined college and Jesuit novitiate, perched on a hill, enjoyed vistas in every direction, especially one overlooking the lake framed by a snow-capped mountain. As the seasons passed, moments multiplied when you stopped to be riveted by the view. Surely this was not New York State but an Alpine Plateau in possession of the undulating hills.

That day the college was on holiday schedule to celebrate the feast of the Jesuit founder, St. Ignatius. As an incoming novice already settled in my room, I had been assigned to set up the dining room for dinner, which promised to be a procession of food from hors d'oeuvres to dessert. After a quick lunch, I changed into a T-shirt and shorts eager to get outside and enjoy the Indian summer. I found myself in the company of a second year novice, Jay Carlisle, who had also helped out in the dining room. Earlier we had planned to go to the lake, change into bathing suits, and test the water. It was now or never; in a few weeks the temperature would plunge and make the lake unswimmable. Jay and I rushed out the door and took the steps in twos competing to get to ground level.

It was then I saw Nathan—white shorts and sneakers, a striped polo, a cable-knit sweater draped over shoulders: it was a congenial outfit worn with an insouciant air. He carried a racket in his left hand and with his right gestured to his companion who laughed aloud. They both approached and stopped to hear Jay introduce me as a first year novice. Nathan lowered his gaze. More intent on listening than observing, his manner was one to which I would soon grow accustomed. His face was flushed from tennis while his wet polo, clinging to his torso, revealed a swimmer's muscular build. Streaked blond hair, green eyes, and a fair complexion completed the Aryan good looks. Striking without being classically handsome, he impressed me as having vitality always on tap. He stood a little apart, less remote than curious, like a visitor from the heights testing life in the plains below. In those days, if we were all aspiring Olympians, Nathan was one by natural affinity.

"How did it go?" Jay asked Nathan.

"How did what go?"

"Tennis."

Nathan's companion, Tim Shalvey, answered for him.

"He won both games. Nathan's serve is deadly. His corner shots are equally lethal. He plays the way he writes poems." He added, "Nothing is wasted."

Jay looked at me, then back at Nathan who was grinning.

"You and Joseph should get together. He writes poetry too."

I blushed. Jay saw the poem I was reworking when he had burst in to my room earlier that morning.

"What kind of poetry?" Nathan asked.

"I suppose you'd call it formal. I play with verse forms and then do something with them."

"So you make them your own?"

"Yes."

"Formalities are good. Without them, some poems resemble tennis without a net. There's nothing to make you thrill. I'd enjoy seeing one."

Smiling, he gave a barely perceptible nod as if he were dismissing himself and us. He and Tim crossed the lawn while Jay and I took the path to the lake.

"I'd love to be a fly on the wall for that one."

"For what?" I asked.

"For the conversation between you and Nathan. You'll find him charming and distant at the same time. Whether it's intentional or not, he cultivates a sphinx-like bearing. And he does things out of the blue. Watch him at the lake. He'll run along the shoreline kicking the waves. Then suddenly, when you least expect it, he dives in and vanishes only to show up in back of you."

"Is his poetry accessible?"

"I'm not the one to ask. Try Tim. He says Nathan is obsessed with precision. He'll get up in the middle of the night to change a word. He has a passion for perfection, no matter what it costs."

"How would Tim know?"

"We're a small enough seminary, Joseph. Stories get around. Soon you learn who the golden boys are. Nathan is one of the luminaries."

I heard nothing about him until the following week when Jay approached me during recreation in a state of excitement. He liked being the harbinger of gossip and was in possession of a juicy piece.

"Joseph, did you hear what happened to Nathan last night?"

"No. I took an early sleep and was out cold."

"Nathan was absent from litanies and night visit. I found out later he had lost track of time because he was working on a poem. At nine forty-five, when he realized how late it was, he left his room but found he was in a dark corridor. The lights at his end were out, except for one near the stairwell. The darkness resulted from a bad circuit breaker. As Nathan walked to the main stairs, an enormous figure came out of nowhere. He wore a black cape over broad shoulders and the shadow he cast was huge. Nathan screamed as the shape approached. A basso voice with Hungarian accent reassured him: 'Do not be afraid. It is I, Radanyi.'"

"Who?" I asked.

"Rocco Radanyi. He's new to the faculty. He's an expatriate from the Hungarian Jesuits who were ousted by the Communists. He's six foot one and weighs over two hundred pounds. With his black cape he looked like Count Dracula."

"Nathan must have laughed when he learned who it was."

"Not really. He fainted. Radanyi tried reviving him. Opening his eyes, Nathan kicked him away and fainted again. When he came to, he was in his room with the lights on and several of us looking down. We had carried him in."

Those are my first full memories of Nathan Darcie. Who could have guessed they would be remembered five decades later by a scholar of Buddhism!

Throughout August and early September, I saw Darcie but we scarcely acknowledged each other. While he was in juniorate, a second year rhetorician, I was a novice in first year novitiate. We were both "on grades." This phrase enjoined a complete disengagement; in brief, we were forbidden each other's company in thought, word, and deed. Nathan was reading Latin and Greek classics together with British and American literature; I was confined to studying the prerequisites of Jesuit life and attending conferences by the novice master. The only books available to me were hagiography whose fanciful stories about mendicants, missionaries, and martyrs stretched belief to the elastic limit. After first vows everything would change, for it was not till I became a junior that the apartheid of grades would cease. I still had a long road to travel.

In mid-September there began the thirty-day retreat, the first test of a genuine Jesuit vocation; it did not terminate until mid-October. With its stretches of silence and solitude, its multiple hours of prayer, and the absence of overt socializing, it was enough to tax the fervor of any eighteen-year-old. I had the misfortune of catching poison ivy during an afternoon of clearing underbrush from the main road. After days of involuntary scratching, aggravated by an Indian summer and a wool habit, I had spread the rash to most of my body and was forced to see the infirmarian. Thus began the assault of calamine lotion on my suppurating sores. I remember hearing from the pulpit how Christ had cured nine lepers. Everyone seemed to glance at me. I looked like a ghost for I was swathed from neck to foot in the pink lotion which, when dry, cracked, and flaked. The one thing missing in my humiliation was a leper's rattle that warned the populace I was approaching. The skin rash came and went with the long retreat. The next time Nathan and I could fraternize was the day I received permission to be off grades. It was October 19, the feast of the Jesuit North American Martyrs, and a week after the retreat had ended. At Nathan's suggestion, I had left him not one but two poems which he said would spark our conversation. He replied by taping a note to my door:

"I'll pack a lunch. We can eat overlooking the lake. Meet me on the loading platform at one o'clock."

We had walked for a half hour on a path that cut through the woods. I was careful to avoid the underbrush, loath to repeat a second bout with poison ivy. I recognized the shape of the leaf and its shiny green surface, and I was savvy enough not to touch my shoes when later I removed them. We came to a break in the trees. In front of us, the grassy ledge, large enough for two people to sit, looked out on the lake's vast expanse a hundred feet below. The trees clustered on the horizon were in their autumnal beauty: red, burnished gold, and some already edging to burnt sienna. We had ventured forth at the height of the season. The sun was bright in a cloudless sky, and the winds when they came in gusts softly buffeted the face.

The chicken salad sandwiches were delicious, and Nathan had brought along apples for dessert. I ate with gusto while I heard him discuss my two poems as if they were selections from my collected works. He spoke in rounded sentences like a poet laureate who knew his craft in theory and practice:

"You have some solid poems here, Joseph. They have a superb sense of tone, perhaps the hardest thing to catch in words. A general weakness is in not making the language the inevitable and utterly achieved word you're looking for. But this is a mastery that comes through long practice."

"So you think I should continue writing?"

"Yes. You've made an admirable start in conceiving images with a tone ready-made. But in choosing language, you'll want to show less strain or self-consciousness; get more ease and directness. A help in improving imagery will be to strive for coherence in the poem's overall structure.

The discipline of rhyme and meter will ensure the music. So keep up the fine writing, Joseph. Just remember—and I remind myself daily—it's hard work being a poet."

Nathan reached into his bag and handed me my two poems along with a typed sheet:

"Here are some jottings. I didn't want to write on your pages. When I do I spill red ink in hopeless profusion."

Eager to see what he had written, I disciplined my curiosity and put his comments in my backpack. Later in my room, I studied his words till they were committed to memory. I offer the reader both poems and their commentaries.

At Norwich

My barren soul was seasoned
By winter, wizened and crone,
Till one day, Love
Gave warmth to it,
Making yield
The flint and stone
To a fallow field.

"Now agile am I as the leaf day-long,
Dancing the breeze for song"

Here miracles fall
Like flower chips;
Words lighter than dreams
Escape from my lips
As into enchanted sleep
The quick heart's beat

Slips into prayer,
More deep than stellar silence,
More subtle than touch of air.

"Do not tremble nor start to weep,
This is how the angels sleep."

Such is the infinite guile of grace
That Father speaks Word
From Julian's face.

At Norwich: I think your diction is too self-conscious through inversion, despite the fact that a taut style for such a subject may have special value. The problem of language is a difficult one, and concentration in the manner of Hopkins presupposes intense emotion on the author's part. But the imagery is impressive throughout. The two intervening couplets are excellent, and the last three lines arresting indeed. In these instances which I praise, the language is accomplished.

The Prodigy

I

White kindle wood
Bursts into flame,
And warm rain stirs
In the pendulous rose.

II

I am child turned sculptress,
See me ply my chisel and mallet,

While every taste of bread, sip of wine,
Moulds my body's image,
Makes him mine.

Night or day
I go dreaming:
    With coral chips
    I'll color his lips,
    Compose his voice a leitmotif
    Blithe as the rustled leaf.
    I'll ravel a skein of stars
    From the winter skies:
    Their light will thread my loom
    To weave his eyes.

O infant:
    But borrow my maidenhood
    From me,
    And hear miraculously
    Fountaining motherhood.

III

Three seasons' leavening
Since first I clutched
Your womb,
Then passed beyond your Easter tomb,
Stone untouched.

Every hour,
I climbed your lofty tower,

Going as the bee to blossoms,
Full and pink
Tugging their buds for drink.

O prodigy of mother:
Later, measure my love by pain at heart
(This infant peace is fragile)
And know, in love, you are my counterpart.

The Prodigy: The conception of this is lovely, and the imagery carries it well—to this extent, at least—that it is sharp and alerts the reader. But here again one might ask if the images develop the total poem as coherently as you'd wish. For example, the three arts of sculpture, painting, and weaving are used early and mixed, one of them with bread and wine. The third stanza recalls the bread, and then moves into an image of the bee to suggest nursing. Now this kind of wandering tends to disconnect images and render them more fanciful than revelatory of meaning. Nonetheless, I think this poem has a fine sense of rhythm, and the link of Mary's virginal birth with Christ's Resurrection is theologically startling.

Although this typed sheet is mottled with age, the remarks are as fresh today as when written fifty years ago.

It is thus I like to remember Nathan as we sat that day on a grassy knoll overlooking the lake discussing poetry, and throughout my first year: Nathan kneeling in a pew reserved for juniors to the chapel's right, his eyes closed and his mind absorbed less by prayer than by poetry; Nathan at the philosophate when he received a D from Father William Noon, his English professor, for sarcastically defining Gongorism—an ornate literary style—as a form of Spanish syphilis; Nathan with his habit open at the neck, looking sullen and unhappy, hating philosophy and showing it by being sent down in his orals; Nathan biting hard on a cigarette like a clerical Kerouac as he revised a poem; or performing at midnight a forbidden dive into the seminary pool; Nathan at a chance meeting on Fordham's campus after he had left the Jesuits, and the "Four hours we spoke, oblivious that time/Had ticked the evening passed in offbeat rhyme." Before I heard his name again, five decades would pass when the dikes would open and the seminary years inundate me in a flood of memories.

The day after my return from Italy, Scott Batey and I sat at a corner table in Dean & Deluca. We had finished our lunch and were sipping double espressos. Whatever the effects of jet lag that morning, they yielded now to black coffee and rapt attention to Scott's words. The account of my summer travels paled in comparison with his enthusiasm for Nathan's play. He cited liberally from the rave reviews:

"Joseph, listen to this one: 'This play is as potent a drama about the effects of war as I've ever seen; an indictment of the senseless brutality our own generation is unable to escape. It's so raw that it's almost hard to bear, watching it in the confines of a theater. The work is stunning, for we are reminded of truths we keep forgetting, namely, that the victims of war are everybody; that all of humanity is diminished by it. With thousands of American soldiers returning from Iraq, this play is timely, but it transcends a single conflict, for it focuses on the tragic and inevitable toll on human lives.' Or this one: 'This is a highly charged explosive play that reveals how the violence of distant war affects the heart of America. It is a sublime disquisition on the role of heroism and the healing power of friendship and community. It is in tune with our concerns for returning veterans from Iraq and Afghanistan. We are grateful to this reclusive former Jesuit for his long-awaited play written over a period of ten years.'"

"I could read other citations, Joseph, but I won't bore you with repetitive excellence. Nathan has clearly done it this time. I wish you had been there. There was a standing ovation and even cheering from the audience as the small cast of actors came out to receive the applause. I counted three curtain calls."

"I wonder what Nathan is doing now."

"Why not try to reach him? It's been a while since you two have talked, but you have more than enough to break the silence."

Scott handed me copies of the two reviews and returned to NYU for an afternoon class. I returned to my apartment and began my sleuthing for information. What follows is the epistolary exchange Nathan and I had as a result of my luck in finding him.

5 January 2007

Dear Nathan:

It seems odd to be writing you after so many years. But I returned from Italy to learn your most recent play had been performed not far from where I live. I would like to have seen it, especially since it received such superb reviews in all the local papers. I missed the last performance by two days. Congratulations on your achievement.

Is there any way I can retrieve the text? I would happily pay for the privilege. I made inquiries at the Drama Bookstore in New York but without success. Perhaps you can suggest a procedure for getting access.

Along with college teaching, I'm also involved in writing. So I know the commitment that goes into producing memorable language at the level of mastery in your newest play. I'm not surprised. I remember you as one of the stellar writers at Bellarmine College, and the few conversations with you I was permitted encouraged my efforts to write seriously. You were the pioneer.

It would please me to initiate a correspondence. But I do not know your e-mail address. In fact, trying to hunt you down took some doing. Then I recalled a biographical note and the words Las Vegas that appeared in a review of your play. I phoned information for that city and found you were listed with a corresponding address. I praised my luck in finding you accessible. I called you once, leaving a message, but thought it best to follow up with the written word. I knew you would prefer it.

I hope you're in good health and thriving. I wish you the best for 2007. Along with fond memories, you have my warm regards,

Joseph

14 January 2007

Dear Joseph,

How surprising to hear from you after nearly half a century! I hope this has reached you, since you didn't mention your zip code. I don't have a computer, nor do I plan to get one, hence no e-mail.

The play had a limited engagement. I'm sorry you missed attending a performance, though you live nearby. The director has copies of the script, but he's using them to explore the possibility of other productions. All I have now is my master copy, having sent the one other copy to a scholar at Oxford, who's including a study of the play in a forthcoming book to be published by the university press.

You don't say what kind of writing you're engaged in, but I certainly wish you well with it. I'm now absorbed by a fresh project on a demanding schedule, which leaves me little time for anything else. I appreciate your kind words, both about my play and the times at Bellarmine.

Cordially,

Nathan

P.S. I addressed you as "Mr." on the envelope, since, for some reason, I assumed you're no longer in the Society. Pardon me, if I'm wrong.

22 January 2007

Dear Nathan:

Your letter arrived a little late because of the absence of zip code. My lapse. But I was pleased to get news of you and to hear more about the play. Marvelous that Oxford sees fit to publish. The superlatives the play garnered during its brief run are reason enough.

I'm enclosing a biography from my website. Yes, I'm a priest but no longer a Jesuit. I'm an extern member of an SJ community in which Dan Berrigan lives; hence, my fond association. I function out of NY as a chaplain at an archdiocesan nursing home where I preach and say Mass each Sunday. My mother lived there until her death at almost 99. I am devoted to the Carmelite sisters who run the establishment.

I've been professor of Buddhism at Fordham and on the summer faculty of a college in Lugano, Switzerland, where I've taught the summer session. The comparative religious teaching helps to finance forays into fiction, my first secular love.

I'm including some poetry which I wrote during our time at Bellarmine College, when you were a rhetorician, and I was a novice. The dedication is original to the poem. I thought I would send it along for your serious amusement. I considered you to be the most gifted poet the college produced, and I recall with pleasure the controversial poems you published in "The Philosopher" during the incarcerated Shrub Oak years. I'm sorry I did not keep copies. Apart from their emotive power, I thought them so skillful in balancing thought with metric form.

I would happily send on an inscribed novel, *Portrait of a Woman*, about a novelist who falls in love with an older woman in his imagination. He then writes a novel (within the novel) about what it would have been like to love her as a contemporary. Chinese boxes, you ask. Yes, several.

I'm clear about your discipline in writing. The word "recluse" in one review clinched for me the rigor with which you conduct your life. Good if it gives us more plays.

Should you ever come to NYC for whatever reason, it would please me to take us to dinner. I have several wines from which to choose to toast your recent success.

Thank you for taking the time to write. Let me finish by saying that I remember our walking conversations *con tanto piacere.*

With warm regards,
Joseph

P.S. Here is the poem which I wrote at Bellarmine College. I had to smile at the bravado in the closing lines. Doubtless, they'll provoke a similar smile in you.

At Litanies

(for ND)

We knelt together within the secluded church,
Each entertaining some private loveliness;
The clamorous bells impeded the rapid search
For one impeccable word, and left him depressed;
While I, who muttered beside, could not foresee
Behind enfolded fingers and lidded eyes
His desolate mind sought vistas of fantasy
With never an afterthought of the compromise
Enacted between his praying and poetry.

But like a stranded dolphin who daily craves
The old, seductive motions of the sea
And waits to be roused by the summoning of waves,
He longed for the rising image to fluctuate,
Then break into effortless words. Someday he will find
To languish upon that shore was often my fate,
The poet, marooned from his craft, time out of mind.

While others remain content from the twilight's start
With paltry stars that shed but a meager light,
We two, expansive of mind and restless at heart,
Would catch in our words whole galaxies of night.

1 February 2007

Dear Joseph,

I see from your biographical sketch that you earned all
the academic buttons, for which congratulations! And you've

certainly been a prolific writer. If I find extended leisure this summer, I'll ask you to send me a novel, but as I mentioned, a large project is underway, and at this age with time short and energy not as it was, I know my limits. Making promises about the future is only matched by the difficulty of unraveling the past. You were kind about my *juvenalia*. I've read your remarkable poem several times, though I'm sure it will take still more till I fully delve it.

You asked in your earlier phone call about Shalvey. He lives ten minutes away. While his being out here wasn't the chief reason for my move, it made the transition to a warmer clime easier. It's true I am a cenobite but one without religious affiliation. This hermitage has only a single occupant. Still, the imagination keeps it populated enough. Continued success with your fiction, stage work, and lecturing. Your zest for it all is enviable.

Cordially as ever,

Nathan

P.S. Grant Davis is teaching a course similar to yours at Tulane in New Orleans. You might want to look him up and compare.

20 February 2007

Dear Joseph,

Make that "*juvenilia.*" Oh, well, it's what comes of relying on memory at this age. But it gives me an opportunity again to congratulate you on all your good works and send best wishes.

25 February 2007

Dear Nathan:

I returned from the US Virgin Islands, St. John, to find your Monet postcard with its acknowledgment of an erratum. Only someone with your meticulous sense would take the time to correct what, quite frankly, went unnoticed. I had to smile at your candor. Truth, they say, is in the detail, and I marvel at such precision all but dead in most quarters. You have Evelyn Waugh's instinct for treating lapses of spelling and grammar as (almost) moral issues.

Since you've mentioned *juvenilia*, I have a request. Would it be possible to ask for a poem from your "juvenile" period? You needn't say yes, and I won't be offended if you don't send one. But it would be appreciated. I'm assuming you have copies, but you may have, like Hopkins, consigned them to the dustbin. If you do and are thus inclined, it would help me revisit a forgotten pleasure. I'll send on *Portrait* when your schedule invites diversion.

Warm regards,
Joseph

15 March 2007

Dear Joseph,

Again, I wish I had time to reply in kind to your letter or could even summon enough interest in my early lyrics to hunt them down, but I trust you will understand and accept my continued good wishes for your original writing, which must be a sustaining delight.

Cordially,
Nathan

Several months passed since receiving this last reply from Nathan. The silence was unsettling especially since I had mailed him a copy of his poems from Fordham's archives. I received no reply from him either of pleasure, reluctance, or gratitude. So I wrote an ex-Jesuit from Nathan's year, and shared my concern that was fast becoming anxiety. Perhaps, in the interim, Grant Davis had heard something. I received this answer:

Joseph,

I have not written Nathan Darcie in more than a year, and your implied anxiety about health and death is contagious, especially as he nears his eighth decade. Nathan and I have written each other every eighteen months or so, and like you, I suddenly worried if he's still alive. It's like mail in the era of sailing ships when a round trip was measured in years. But that's the way it's been. Nathan, as we both recall, intentionally or unintentionally fostered an attitude of remoteness, and I suspect something similar at present. I hesitate to suggest anything. I recognize his possible preferences, and worry both that he may be disabled or may simply be pulling his hermit routine initiated so many years ago. He once mentioned in a letter that he found the phone "frightening," and I have respected that ever since. Like you, I read about his play's off-Broadway production, and was mortified that I did not support it. But my teaching rarely allows me to get north of the Mason-Dixon Line.

Regards,
Grant Davis

I've decided to follow Grant's lead and respect Nathan's privacy, whatever the reason: temperamental or literary. He has made it known politely that he wants to be left alone. I will not test this choice. In reading our correspondence, I see that he has both the benefits and drawbacks of the recluse; while not fearful of life, he will "always stand at a slight angle to the universe" (E. M. Forster). Which, then, is more advantageous, the company of others or solitude? As a former Jesuit, Darcie understands the value of both and so might answer, "I'm not aware that I have to choose." If his recent play is any proof, he has managed a posture of disinterested caring by being in the world but not of it. This much is clear: such a life is not for the faint-hearted but demands a resolute spirit. So Nathan, my friend, long may you thrive and "toughly I hope you may thole" (John Crowe Ransom).

The years in Jesuit seminaries were memorable because I was privileged to live in close association with gifted persons like Nathan Darcie. Those without his imaginative brilliance directed their speculative talents toward philosophy, theology, or literary studies. What we all shared in common was a commitment to the Jesuit order whose spirit was epitomized in its constitutions and rule. Despite wide variations in aptitude, a shared vision bound us together. Whatever our career choices, the Jesuit priesthood was our future goal and inspiration. Toward it we all moved steadily and by stages. The homily at my first Mass reflects the joy at having arrived.

Ordination Homily

Mom and Dad, Joan and Michael; Reverend Fathers and Sisters of St. Mark's; my fellow Jesuits, relatives, friends, and parishioners:

With joy and satisfaction I have come here this afternoon to celebrate my first Mass as a Jesuit priest. In so doing, I'm expressing publicly my new relationship to you as Christ's minister in word and sacrament. That I should return to St. Mark's is fitting. Here I first felt the stirrings of a priestly vocation some twenty-five years ago when I was enrolled as a student in the parish school. Here the Dominican Sisters challenged an inquiring mind and directed it toward those great truths which are the heritage of Catholic Christianity.

My response to the Sisters is fond affection whenever memories of St. Mark's claim my attention. I remember the starched linen of their veils and the scent of lemon oil on the classroom floors. I recall the spontaneous obedience they received ranging from folded hands on the desk to perfect genuflections in church. So deep are these impressions that to this day I cannot look at white linen without the faint recollection of something Dominican. And while the Jesuits won my adolescent allegiance, it could never have happened had the Sisters of St. Dominic not preceded them. Like John the Baptist, they were the forerunners. They guided my way even when my willfulness made them resemble voices crying in the desert.

The Dominicans were not alone in shaping my life. Those early years were dominated by the two-source theory of Catholicism: the convent and the rectory. When I recall St. Mark's rectory in the fifties, Fathers Kiernan, Lahey, McKenna, and Termine crowd my memories. Because of them this altar is no stranger. In those years when as a fledgling altar boy I stumbled through the Latin of the Confiteor, rang the bells prematurely at the Sanctus, or tripped on my cassock in the perilous ascent from Epistle to Gospel side, I felt supported like Jeremiah in our first reading: "My friends are on the watch for any misstep of mine."

Of the Jesuits it is more difficult for me to speak, as difficult as a married person expressing the complex meaning of a marital commitment; it is tried at the risk of saying too much or too little. Something so intimate cannot be addressed but only felt. Still, when I think of that vast Company of Jesus scattered throughout the world in a hundred different countries, exercising to God's greater glory a hundred occupations—from measuring solar eclipses to juggling oranges in a circus—I stand amazed at the output of imagination and intelligence; more so, I feel safe with an unassailable security. Because the Jesuits are there, I am here at home with myself, with family and friends, and with God. Like King David in the responsorial psalm, I lift up my heart and say, "Bounteous is your kindness, Lord. In your great love you have answered me."

In the spirit of the Gospel reading, I would like to speak of my parents: to declare in the light what I've heard in darkness, and proclaim from the rooftops what I've learned in private. In preparing for ordination, I have spent hours reflecting on them and their role in my life, and have turned for clarity to my most immediate evidence: to my sister, brother, and myself. We have stepped out from them as images from a mirror. If we three have earned the esteem of friends and colleagues for intelligence, humor, and good judgment, these qualities would not have been possible without my parents' struggle to surmount the most stubborn obstacles.

From my mother we learned the fine art of precision, of doing things with tenacity, fairness, and an indomitable spirit. From my father we learned how to socialize these qualities by a generous, outgoing manner, and a basic trust in life. This has been our parents' legacy to us: Roman resourcefulness and Sicilian passion running in the bloodline. It's a dicey combination disinclined to smallness or meanness even when it sometimes loses its balance by being impetuous and headstrong. I would not want it otherwise, for it has fostered the desire to live with gusto and fervor; in short, to live memorably.

So here I stand, a quite unfinished man, yet somehow a priest who acknowledges Christ before others so he will not disown me before his Father in heaven. It is a prodigious task, and I'm painfully aware of having been free to choose otherwise. Personal ambition has pressured me to consider alternate futures. The priesthood has risen above all else, risen I say by surprise and in spite of myself. For whenever as a deacon I was summoned to preach a sermon or counsel the confused; explain church doctrine or distribute the Eucharist, I left with a Gospel satisfaction explained best by the words, "Lord, it is good for me to be here." What has resulted is the conviction that my end was in my beginning—what I began years ago—to serve in Christ's church as a priest.

All of you who have borne me and borne with me leave with me today though I must physically leave you. Some of what you taught me I shall rethink and accept, some of it replace; but I can never forget St. Mark's is my place of origin. You are my history; you are part of my self.

On this day of days, I promise to give my best to God and to leave some of it in the world. My closing thoughts are those of Gautama Buddha, who before his death exhorted his followers, "Accomplish the goal with diligence." And after all, his words are not far from the command of Christ, "Be perfect as your heavenly Father."

I delivered this homily on June 22, 1975. Seven years later, I petitioned my superior for release from my Jesuit vows while insisting that I did not seek laicization. "My commitment to the priesthood is irrevocable," I wrote, "even if I believe it cannot be expressed with sincerity in Jesuit religious life." I wrote to Father General in Rome explaining myself in greater detail. I cite at length from this letter dated January 12, 1982:

> After prayerful consideration, it has become clear to me that I can no longer live with a sense of peace in the Society. My reasons are simple: I no longer wish to live Jesuit common life as my Superiors require nor am I inclined to live under the demands of what is canonically meant by religious poverty or Jesuit obedience. I prefer to draw my community from the diverse world at large, Christian and non-Christian. I wish to take on myself the responsibilities of self-support and residence outside the constraints of religious permission, and to do so as

good judgment dictates. Permit me to add that my commitment
to service in the Church implied by the spirit of celibacy
remains unchanged.

In rereading this letter, I hear the intransigence in my attitude. It's
clear I wanted my life on my own terms. Something major had happened
in the interim between an ordination homily and this decision. Was it a
young priest's version of the seven year itch? Did my agitation come from
raging hormones during graduate studies and the easy means around me
to assuage them? Or was it my joyless stay in Bangkok and the terror of
residing in communities governed by a barracks mentality? What I do know
is that my departure from the order preceded several other leave-takings:
tenure denial from my first teaching appointment and the embarrassment
of vacating the college premises; the absence of money and the need to
be on unemployment; no priestly involvement in pastoral care. Soon I
would face my brother's illness and the void following his death. For the
time-being, I was being schooled in the art of detachment. In one of her
poems, Elizabeth Bishop counsels us "to lose something every day." I
was following her advice with a vengeance. My slate of identity had been
wiped clean: no functioning priesthood, no teaching assignment, and
no gainful employment. It was then that I started my first novel. It was
another exercise in detachment: no footnotes, no religious or academic
involvement, just engagement with a blank sheet of paper.

What empowered me were my life experiences bolstered by a vivid
imagination. I could now let go without feeling monitored. No one was
observing me or looking over my shoulders. Without constraints the words
came in a torrent of fluency and surmounted the levees that for years had
hemmed them in. The pedagogy of loss had cleared the decks and left me
on my own. In a state of receptivity I discovered what I wanted to be: a
fiction writer. My life at the behest of the word was supported by years of

writing poetry in which I honed the art of precision. Each day I packed my attaché with paper, fountain pens, and ink, and found a café where I wrote without distraction. The book was a fictional version of my doctoral thesis, a novel I called *Fire in a Windless Place*. The silence, solitude, and concentration enjoined in the seminary were all focused on composing my love story in Bangkok. It was still asceticism but one pressed into the service of literature.

During the frustrating years of seeking a literary agent, of dealing with obtuse publishers who applauded my plots but dismissed their religious ideas, I functioned as a priest at Loyola University, Chicago. There for twenty summers I taught comparative religion in the Institute of Pastoral Studies. Its diverse program educated adults for ministerial leadership. Through classroom seminars and theological formation, the students developed skills in pastoral work and contemporary ethics. The institute was largely the brainchild of a brilliant educator, Jerry O'Leary, a Dominican from the mid-West, whom I met by accident when he was staying with the Jesuits at John La Farge House in Cambridge. I had just received my PhD, and Jerry was eager to tap my doctoral freshness.

"Why not come to Loyola? You can lecture on Buddhism and see how the students react. I'll send you a plane ticket, and there's a stipend to encourage your visit." As a second generation Sicilian, I knew he had made me an offer I couldn't refuse.

So I went and kept going for two decades as an adjunct professor. And oh, what a paradise it was. Jerry had a genius for gathering astute but idiosyncratic people whose backgrounds were as resonant as their lives. Together they made up a full orchestra, and I was now a player adding to the huge sound. I found a congenial faculty who daily displayed their wit at The Breakfast Club and then later at The Cocktail Hour. Peter

Gilmour, Jim Halstead, Jim and Evelyn Whitehead, Patricia Killen, Lucian and Barbara Roy, and preeminently, Richard Woods were some of the virtuosos. Richard was my contemporary, a Dominican priest by commitment and a connoisseur of knowledge. It was a feast being in his studied company, for his range of secular interests was matched only by his knowledge of mysticism. How could I not be impressed? To this day he remains an engaging friend. When through his auspices my play, *Waging Waugh*, was performed at the university theater to enthusiastic reviews, I decided that if it ever reached book form, I would dedicate it to him. Published in 2009, I kept my promise: "For Rev. Richard J. Woods, OP, *eloquentiae semper laudator.*"

On Loyola's campus I heard confessions and preached at the university church of Madonna della Strada. Though I had left the New York Jesuits, Chicago's Society of Jesus welcomed me with full faculties to function pastorally. When I wasn't teaching, I enjoyed Chicago's cultural offerings, which flourished during the summer. I was living in the dorm assigned to visiting faculty. It had no air-conditioning to ease the sultry weather, which alternated with arctic temperatures in the classroom. So went the oscillation and it wore me out. I was back in Bangkok where dripping humidity alternated with fixes in air-conditioned hotels. My situation changed when I explained to Jerry O'Leary I wasn't sleeping. Immediately he arranged to have me reside at the Jesuit residence whose amenities suited my needs. I began to look human as I lost the somnambulist's stare, and I returned to the bonhomie of afternoon cocktails.

It was there I met David and Char. He was a doctoral candidate in the throes of finishing a degree while his wife was a teacher with an active imagination. Both charming and good-looking, I surmised why Jerry had added them to the growing orchestra. Body, brains, and benevolence were an assured combination to entice his attention. David and Char enjoyed my New York sassiness. One afternoon at drinks, as David looked on, Char asked me:

"Joseph, would you join us at Grant Park for the Friday concert? David and I plan to go, and it would be fun to have you along."

The invitation was flattering; I was also free.

"Yes," I said without hesitation.

"Good. After Friday's cocktail hour, we'll drive over to the park and stake out our claim."

The evening ran the gamut from good food to even better conversation. The orchestra's music, although at a distance, was piped through speakers judiciously placed around the park. The musical selections were crowd-pleasers: Tchaikovsky, Strauss, John Philip Souza followed by a medley of Beatles music. Char had set out a picnic of salads: chicken, salmon, shrimp, and potato. Quaffable wines—Chablis and Riesling—were well paired, and their low alcohol content respected our awareness.

Breezes from the lake punctuated the warm evening. Teenage couples who sat amiably alongside were rolling cigarettes and smoking them. They exhaled in billowing clouds while the smoke wafted in my direction. *It's rather pleasant*, I thought, *a cognac base with an enhancing spice*. As they smoked, I closed my eyes while inhaling the haze. The arrangement went undisturbed till I heard Char and David address me. I did not reply. In the midst of the smoke I was too busy grinning. As the smoke surrounded me, my grin became laughter. I giggled as if a feather were grazing my underarm. Char and David shared my amusement, remarking how well placed we were on the grass.

I don't remember leaving the concert. I do recall dozing in the back of a car, arriving at my door, and being helped to my room. I awoke the next morning still dressed and lying on my bed. With lucidity at its low point, I held my head and groaned. Why was I fully clothed flat on my back? Who put me there? Bolting upright, I suddenly remembered, then toppled over like a domino. This is my first and only account how on a blanket in grassy Grant Park I got stoned.

When I wasn't teaching summers in Chicago, I was back in Manhattan helping out as chaplain at Cabrini Medical. I presided at a televised Mass each Saturday for the residents and medical community, and afterward I attended to those critically ill with AIDS. The archdiocese permitted this ministry without pressing me to incardinate; I was doing work for which no priest had volunteered. It helped that I took no stipend. I was not pressured to live in a rectory. My situation resembled that of three British priests: Ronald Knox, Robert Hugh Benson, and Alfred Gilbey. Each was ordained a priest "under his own patrimony." As men of independent means they were not subject to a diocesan bishop's jurisdiction. Each retained responsibility for his own maintenance, instead of being sponsored by a bishop and incardinated into a diocese. Private means, especially in the case of Monsignor Gilbey, allowed them to enjoy freedom from parochial employment. Like myself all three were writers, and in the case of Robert Hugh Benson—the convert son of the archbishop of Canterbury—a novelist of reputation. During his lifetime Ronald Knox's Bible translation enjoyed wide currency. Arthur Gilbey of the Gin family used his money to finance the chaplaincy at Fisher House in Cambridge University, and had it furnished to the standards of a gentleman's club. There he wittily held court mentoring the undergraduates in Catholic doctrine and practice. A well-stocked wine cellar enlivened their instruction.

An emeritus abbot and an astute canon lawyer have told me that I too function under my own patrimony since my departure from the Jesuits occurred in 1982 when the canonical privilege was still intact. So I have a freedom of choice allowed me by the diocesan administrator of Priest Personnel. I'm left blissfully alone to live where I choose, and minister where I'm needed. Of these three who enjoyed their own patrimony, I find myself a surprising fourth.

Though not by temperament a docile person, I'm susceptible to the advice of friends who have my interests at heart. After my brother's death in 1986, Father Daniel Berrigan recommended I reconnect with his community of Jesuits; I acceded to his suggestion and joined them for Mass and dinner, theological discussion, and group retreats. Eventually, I found myself with a card-carrying membership in which "Jesuit" was inscribed not *de jure* but *de facto*. Father Frederick O'Connor, the oldest member of the community, put it succinctly one evening when we met in the elevator going to the eighth floor for dinner: "Joe," he said, "you're one of us." This pithy remark was later reinforced when the former provincial of the New Orleans province suggested to me: "Why not come back and finish what you started?" So in easy stages I followed their advice by taking a room in the community. I shuttled back and forth to visit my mother's apartment, checked on her health, and then left for Fordham where I taught in the global studies program. Zigzagging from downtown and midtown to uptown, I had the air of one perpetually catching trains.

During one summer retreat, the assembled West Side Jesuits without exception urged me to reapply. I wrote the New York provincial a letter in which I asked that my talents "be returned to the Jesuits where they belong so the Society receives credit for them." I added: "I do not believe I will crumble if faced with a negative judgment. Over the years I have developed a strong trust in providence." Months later I received the following reply from the provincial:

> In reflecting more fully on this subject, I have become more convinced of the validity of my initial conclusion that it would be unwise for you to be readmitted to the Society. This decision has been a difficult one since I have a great deal of affection and admiration for you and for your ministry. I know well your own care for the Society and for your many Jesuit friends. I am convinced, nevertheless, that your current work and ministry—with its own set of personal and professional

demands—can be best done outside the Society while maintaining strong bonds of friendship and affection for the many Jesuits you know and admire.

He added that "this decision may not be easy for you to hear," and it was not. While his refusal disappointed me—and the West Side Jesuits as well—I have come to agree with his judgment. His reading of my situation was correct. As a result of living on my own, I had altered my view of religious life. I did not think myself completely misaligned. Despite a growing disinclination toward poverty, chastity, and obedience, I still had a naturally Jesuit temperament. Even my novel, *The Odor of Sanctity*, written in the fervor of possible reentrance, did not sustain the alliance. I cite the novel's plot on the front flap:

A priest, Jewish convert, and practicing psychiatrist, Peter Albright is called to make Final Vows in the Jesuit Order. What happens when he learns his grandfather, murdered at Auschwitz, has left him a fortune in an anonymous, unnumbered Swiss account is the heart of this timely novel. Should Peter pursue his fortune and how? His major clues are the odors of scented stationery. His major complication is the perfume expert, a beautiful woman offering help, then falling in love. Religious commitment and the lure of millions, romantic love and the call to priesthood all play out against the terrible odds of dead ancestors and the Holocaust remembered. The reader is drawn to these conflicts as though to fireworks where explosions displace one another, each more dazzling than the last. How Peter decides makes THE ODOR OF SANCTITY not only a suspenseful page-turner but a study in heroism.

The provincial's letter confirmed my decision to function outside the order. As nostalgic as I was for Peter's commitment, I wanted more the novelist's life. It even superseded my commitment to comparative religion. While I believed writing fiction shared in the ministry of the word, I viewed it as first and foremost. By Jesuit standards, its preeminence rendered me "unmissionable," for I was unable to make the Society's work my principle and foundation. I had become my own order, as it were; its vows were facetiously expressed in *The Devil's Interval* as simplicity, affectivity, and perpetual self-discovery; a fourth was optional for those committed to English, vivid conversation: the vow of never being dull to one's neighbor or oneself.

I sometimes wonder whether, had I not left the Jesuits in 1982, I might have traveled the same road as Father Gerard Manley Hopkins, SJ and arrived at a life divided between literature and priesthood; not resulting in his "terrible" sonnets but a prose darkened by guilt at being caught in a dilemma. I might have endured the same redundant rounds on the academic carousel; not a life of joyous anticipation but one of grim acquiescence as I learned I'd been made: head of a theology department; financial officer for alumni giving; superior of a Jesuit community; president of the university. Jesuits with PhDs from the Ivy League had a marked propensity for landing at the top of the heap because of their gilt-edged credentials. Still, I might have engaged in a less august pedagogy by teaching remedial writing to students whose text messaging had muddled their grammar and garbled their prose; or supervised dissertation topics investigating some fatuous point of religion: "Veiled Imagery in the Gospel of Salome"; "Limbo and Its Vicissitudes"; "Circumcision: Ritual at the Cutting Edge." The freedom to explore a new plot by visiting some exotic locale would have been impossible along with the requisite solitude to shape my findings; even less possible, a published work about a risqué subject without its first being screened by the province censor, since authorship required not just my name but religious initials as well. Did I want the monitoring implicit in SJ?

I remember once being censored for a poem I had penned when I was nineteen years old. Without much warning a novice friend had left the Jesuit novitiate. In a mood of sullen disappointment, I wrote "Outside the Cloister, No Salvation":

> That evening you left us, with casual assertion,
> The black-gowned men examined your quiet desertion:
> "He'll only be happy in retrospect," they said;
> Then, night prayers finished, proceeded securely to bed,
> Content with the delicate balance that carefully joins
> Eloquent scholars to inarticulate loins.
> But in time, when the moderate days are heroic to live,
> Your face will pass through the mind's discriminate sieve
> And offer defense with witty, ironical tongue
> Like wind that scatters the fumes from afternoon dung.

The poem came to the attention of the novice master who summoned me promptly to his room. The manner in which his command was conveyed entailed a tap on my shoulder. Turning around, I acknowledged the gesture that always implied something was gravely wrong. With his second and third fingers, the master's secretary formed a "v." It was short for the Latin word *vult*, "he wishes." The completed thought had a decisive ring: "You're to see him now." The digital sign looked inquisitorial, and I experienced what James Joyce called "that scrotum-tightening feeling." I hastened to the master's room while replaying all my thoughts, words, and deeds of the prior twenty-four hours. *Perhaps,* I guessed, *a minor mishap has befallen a friend.* No such luck. American slang put it colorfully: I was being "called on the carpet" for writing something unworthy of ours. The word translated *nostri*, the plural possessive adjective used substantively for the Society of Jesus: from its foundation in 1540 to its final enthronement at the heavenly court. My poem was an affront to that imposing history. Any creativity by one of ours disparaging the order was forbidden; it amounted to betrayal.

I do not recall the master's words. I'm certain they were a model of *cura personalis* to which we were all enjoined as we "manifested" each other's faults to ensure God's greater glory. But his meaning was clear: no matter how clever or well-written, some forms of expression were never tolerated despite their arguable loss to the world. Art was expendable, the Society of Jesus was not; any detriment to her good name was to be eschewed.

I never published the poem. Now after fifty years it makes its debut. My being summoned in novitiate was a rehearsal for future summonses by other superiors for other reasons. The message was the same: the initials SJ involved prohibitions demanding not just compliance but obedience of mind and will. This was the hallmark of the order.

My mother was an inveterate collector of memorabilia. When in doubt, she filed chronologically and labeled the contents. Consequently, I have all my correspondence with family and friends from 1958 when I entered the Jesuits until 1978 when I earned my doctorate. Twenty years of letters have amounted to hundreds of pages in which no thought of mine seemed to go unrecorded. Like the title of one of my stories, it's "too much of a good thing." Still, I'm grateful my letters were saved. I've read them with the scrutiny of someone examining ancestral selves. In using them as an epistolary guide, I can look back on the preparatory years in the Society and observe an emergent self. Often I resemble a creature eager to be airborne, but inching painfully out of a viscous cocoon. I offer the following remarks like a critic reviewing an episodic film pulled from the archives.

I'm struck by the innocence of those novitiate years from 1958 to 1962. In photos of family visits to Bellarmine College, and the penultimate one after First Vows, I appear supremely happy—and I am. Whatever my determined efforts to be my own person, they were subject to one encompassing goal: being a good Jesuit. I moved in a haze of euphoria, living with my fellow novices on a promontory overlooking

Lake Champlain and Mount Mansfield. Our diversions were long walks, bantering conversation, sports like swimming, biking, tennis, and tobogganing. Our pleasures were basic: a snack on the loading platform; a house play or chorale; holidays on campus or at Port Kent; a bus trip to visit a monastery or to camp in the wilderness. Unencumbered, we were completely focused on the spiritual life as described in the Jesuit rule. Without women, money, technology, newspapers, TV, radio, movies, or dating; with no secular garb except the black habit and cincture and for assigned work, a gray cotton jacket worn over T-shirt and khakis, the multiple choices were minimal. We had made the elimination of fuss into high art. Sacred silence, solitude in one's room, house Latin, fasting or kneeling through meals, long and short retreats were all integral to Jesuit living. We accepted the asceticism with pungent good humor, for we viewed its practice as a residue of the medieval past. We were warned against cliques and romantic friendships. Our rooms were forbidden visits without permission; while outside that inner sanctum, bells summoned us with calculable regularity to Mass, meals, conferences, and litanies. We responded by moving wordlessly with lockstep precision in long black lines.

If novitiate was a time of religious enculturation, it was likewise a period of incubation. If I subtract the years of idyllic adolescence from chronology, it explains why some of us remained boyish into our sixties. Communion with God superseded sexual intimacy which remained in abeyance. At times its urgency made some fall by the wayside. And fall they did in keeping with the novice master's promise to shake the tree and make the loose apples fall.

Still, in the fifties we suffered no decimation of ranks. Camaraderie prevailed from which we drew communal strength. Opportunities arose for individual expression like writing a musical about ecumenism or casting a play about Thomas More. Artful entertainment was a gift made to the community by its members. But no one was touted for solitary brilliance or lauded for singular success. Terse gratitude was given and the triumph passed. There was no reason to enthuse: greatness had happened before, it would happen again. After all, everything was a means to an end. As Ronald Knox has pointed out, *ad majorem Dei gloriam*—to the greater glory of God—involves a kind of "Utilitarianism *in excelsis*" for the furthering of God's kingdom. And if this "holy Philistinism" was an assault on the Renaissance, it was more so on spiritual tepidity. Jesuit life allowed for mediocre results even when you did your best—*age quod agis* in lapidary Latin—but no room existed for mediocre effort. Jesuit history was often "a record of failures that nearly succeeded" like the reductions of Paraguay or the Chinese rites controversy. But the brilliance and folly of these exploits resembled comets lighting up the darkness before sputtering out. It came with the territory.

Juniorate studies from 1960 until 1962 initiated my first two years of college, and gave me unmitigated joy. They felt like a counterblast to my former preoccupation with Jesuit rules, hagiography and history. Classical texts together with English literature became my focus of attention. Exposure to events like Vatican II or the election of John F. Kennedy was greatly expanded, but most expansive of all was access to the library; it became my favorite haunt. Since then, I have never lost the pleasure of browsing through stacks of books. In those two years, I read the Latin works of Horace and Catullus, plowed through Thucydides's Greek history, and felt the rhetorical differences between Euripides and Sophocles as I studied their crisp dialogue or struggled to translate their choruses. My classics professor, a Catholic convert, never cast off his pagan background, and his Catholicism seemed like a ploy to hide from his natural habitat of Olympus. Though we were fresh from vows, he exposed us to any Latin and Greek expurgated from the text. He called on the most proper scholastic to translate the saucy lines. If the English rendering were too refined, he would blurt out the vulgar equivalent and repeat it to make his point: precision must not be sacrificed to prudery. His crudeness made us squirm in our seats.

During those two years, I made poetry a serious commitment and produced a collection called "Poems for Two Violins." Several of my *juvenilia* are included at key moments in my novels, and a limerick translation of Jesus's life has recently been published. Mastering verse forms like the sonnet, the couplet, rime royal, and ottava rima is a superb preparation for writing prose where every word counts. Bull's-eye is preferable not just in archery but in composition. The arrow of precision, drawn from a quiver of words, is chosen to take aim. One shot, one idea. When given a choice of being fanciful or concise, of deleting something beautiful in favor of brevity, I delete every time. I prefer lean sentences to weighty prose.

I play with over a dozen languages which I read more or less proficiently depending on exposure. I have a flypaper's mind for archaic forms and irregular verbs. It's another chance to delight in what's exceptional. If someday illness should confine me, I would return to my Loeb texts and read lyric poetry, glancing at the English only when my Greek vocabulary falters. I share the same predilection as Marguerite Yourcenar who extols ancient Greek in her *Memoirs of Hadrian*:

> I have loved the language for its flexibility, like that of a supple, perfect body, and for the richness of its vocabulary, in which every word bespeaks direct and varied contact with reality: and because almost everything that men have said best has been said in Greek . . . There is nothing to equal the beauty of a Latin votive or burial inscription: those few words graved on stone sum up with majestic impersonality all that the world need ever know of us; my epitaph will be carved in Latin on the walls of my mausoleum beside the Tiber; but it is in Greek that I have thought and lived.

From 1962 to 1965, I studied philosophy at Loyola Seminary in Westchester County. It was a time of raw abstractions couched in Latin theses. I felt pummeled by metaphysics, epistemology, phenomenology, and cosmology. Despite my repugnance for the manner of expression, I studied diligently to prepare for the comprehensive *de universa* exam at the end of three years. My academic career depended on doing well together with my status in the Jesuit hierarchy. I received my Licentiate in Philosophy *magna cum laude*, but not without violence to my imaginative faculty. The spiritual life suffered too; it became increasingly threadbare in fellow seminarians who skipped daily Mass, morning meditation, and night prayer; who threw soirées in their rooms using food and drink squirreled away from feast days. Many played cops and robbers with the house minister responsible for keeping order. He became a smoke detector. We were denied cigarettes because Pius XII had forbidden them to Jesuits. We were warned before entering the order of this papal preference which did not extend to priests already in final vows. For us scholastics in studies, smoking was *verboten*. Adherence to this injunction determined who was obedient and who was "ex lex" or lawless. The minister sniffed for tobacco in the corridors like an SS officer looking for sequestered Jews. Air freshener was ubiquitous. Those who refused to use it were flushed out and reported for their infraction. They knelt at dinner before the whole community to declare their *culpa*. Public penance proved futile, for cigarette recidivism was rife.

Two hundred scholastics from three provinces lived in an environment with no ostensible color: everything was pallid beige. The house chapel had the dimensions of a playing field. The massive crucifix on the high altar loomed over the community and dwarfed us by its magnitude. The corpus of Christ in polished nickel hung against a background of glinting mosaics. Eliciting no warmth, it invited no piety. After a character in an adventure series who rescued lost hikers, we called him Sky King. The chapel became a dead zone and the novitiate habit of slipping in "to make a visit" fell into desuetude.

I recall how a member of the French resistance visited us once to speak of his war experience during the German occupation of Paris. From the questions after, he was convinced young Jesuits grasped perfectly what it meant to live under an oppressor. We concurred with our guest when he insisted he was never freer than under the Nazis. Unlike him we yielded to expedience by substituting verisimilitude for truth.

The community's spiritual father had mastered the phenomenology of restless Jesuits. His conferences addressed compassionately their incarcerated feeling but he offered no way out. Relief came when we were allowed weekly trips to Fordham or St. John's to begin MA programs. Graduate studies broadened our perspective as we sat in class with "secular" students of our own age. The trips failed to help those Jesuits feeling entrapped by the environment. They drank or used tranquilizers to quell the pain. The yen for intimacy was sublimated by working with students whom we taught as regents. That was a year in the future; we were not yet liberated for the apostolate. I recall humming the song: "We gotta get outa this place/If it's the last thing we ever do."

If you read Nathan Darcie's poems published in *The Philosopher*, the seminary's literary magazine, you hear the baptist's voice crying in the desert. I offer the final stanza of "The Grandfather":

> Now every star has delved into the night.
> My lean body cannot be startled—but the fright
> Of not waking has come. Age, do I weep
> For a boy and the thoughts that stagger from his sleep
> Or because I have come with the tide to where I began
> While all his sleeping boyhood has summoned the man?

Nostalgia over a life that has passed and yearning for one unrealized are not the sentiments of one in his twenties. Another poem, *The Actress,* strikes the same note of longing. In the form of a reminiscence, the poem's melancholy is almost unbearable. I give it here in its entirety:

Here, to a home that is not hers, we came.
Performance time, the players, all are the same—
Only the play has been changed. With coffee-dark eyes
We gaze at each other, then at where she lies
In front of the final curtain—recalling the way
she looked receiving flowers after a play.
Now, in what would have been a living room,
we stand like the flowers we sent to bloom
about her body for these two days. Like them,
we still show life and yet, from the cut stem,
we too are dying. Readjusting her shawl,
the sad supporting actress whispers to all,
"How sweetly someone has arranged her hair"
And, "Come for coffee when you've said a prayer."
Moments of sudden silence are like the pause
after a play's last word and before the applause.
On the grey glass of a window the room is reflected.
We pass before the screen where we are projected—
images of indoor artificial light;
reenacting scenes out in the night.

His poems share with Hopkins the dilemma of a split life. Like his predecessor, Nathan dealt with inner conflict. But unlike Hopkins who remained in the order, Nathan left to pursue a playwright's career. His compelling dramas, soon to be anthologized in an Oxford edition, will allow access to his complete corpus.

During regency from 1965 to 1968, I taught French and theology at Brooklyn Prep. I made two trips to France, first with Brooklyn Prep students and then with Utah's Foreign Language League run by the Mormons. My extracurricular activity at prep was the Christian Action Core, a name I coined to replace the Sodality of Our Lady. My language appealed to the young men who were attracted to what I called "kinetic Christianity": to go where the action is. We engaged in social work, ecumenical dialogue, tutoring, and weekend retreats with the girls from the Academy of the Sacred Hearts of Jesus and Mary. Several guitarists, never without their instruments, enlivened our trips. A medley of songs from the Beatles and Simon and Garfunkel, erupting on train stations, attracted passengers to stop and listen.

It was during a stressful period of teaching that Charlie Winans, one of prep's faculty, confronted me. He was still head of the English Department and in charge of dramatics in which I had participated as a senior in 1957. Now he and I were colleagues. He was still an inspiration to those who were exposed to his quirky pedagogy, for he combined the piety of a Francis of Assisi with the selective hedonism of Oscar Wilde. He sounded like no one I have ever met then or since because it was impossible to determine on which side of the Atlantic he belonged. Like the accent of Cary Grant, Charlie's was unique. The story circulated—whether apocrypha or scripture I never learned—that he had corrected a youthful stutter by filling his mouth with marbles and orating grandly into empty air. His thespian's voice combined the plumy richness of John Gielgud with the elegant diction of José Ferrer.

It was Thursday afternoon, late in the spring semester, when Charlie approached me. I had collapsed into a lounge chair in the teachers' room after six periods of teaching the sophomores French and theology. Collectively I called them the coliseum. Again I had fended off the lions of bad grammar and heresy, leaving the amphitheater unscathed but exhausted.

"You look like someone who could use some diversion," he said and then added, "Why not join me for an opera tomorrow at the Met? I have two tickets for *Un ballo in maschera* by Verdi. We can thrill together watching King Gustave get shot. Have you seen it?"

"Never."

"Good. Later we can have supper at a favorite restaurant."

It all sounded perfectly planned. It was typical of Charlie to imagine a scenario in which we both would improvise dramatic parts.

"I think it's what I need," I said without knowing to what I agreed.

"Excellent. I suggest that you leave your clerical collar. Going mufti will be more relaxing. Come to my house on Lincoln Road at 7:00 p.m. and we'll drive to the Met."

I do not recall any details of the opera but supper afterward was unforgettable. Charlie had reserved a table at The Russian Tea Room. I remember approaching the restaurant's velvet ropes that pointed to a revolving door. This in turn led us into a ground floor dining room known for its opulent wall hangings and gorgeous table settings. I had stepped into a czarist reverie as guest of the Romanovs. A waiter who recognized Charlie led us to a red booth framed by spruce green walls.

Charlie ordered for us from the restaurant's savory menu: first cold borscht and then blini that were golden and fluffy. He may have added caviar to the sequence of dishes, but I was too mesmerized by the ambiance to remember. While I drank Chablis, Charlie sipped a cocktail that was his own concoction. Two parts Russian vodka, one part green Chartreuse served over ice in a large brandy snifter, he called it an Ivan the Terrible.

"Would you like a taste?" Charlie asked while nursing his third. I declined. The vapors alone would have had me reeling. The drinks did not deter his conversation, for the layered prose rolled off his tongue. He spoke fondly of Czar Nicholas as if the two had been classmates. Occasionally, I flashed a glance at my watch; it was eleven thirty and Charlie was in no hurry to abort the festive evening. I was mentally framing my words about getting home, when he interrupted my thoughts:

"Would you mind accompanying me to pick up a friend? Ron phoned just before we left for the opera, and I said I would oblige."

"Not at all," I answered using a Jesuit mental reservation.

Charlie called for the check, paid it, and we were presently out on the street driving to pick up Ron Hershman, a student friend. He often bunked at Charlie's house whenever he came to New York. All I knew of Ron was that he was finishing a doctorate in English literature.

"It will take a little time," Charlie said to my consternation.

Now close to midnight, I imagined myself walking into prep in the wee hours, taking the stairs to my floor, and bumping into the rector, Father Jack Morrison. He was known to patrol the corridors at odd hours. Rumor had it that as a former army chaplain, he kept a gun in his top drawer and was not averse to using it.

"May I ask where we're going?"

"The University of Delaware," Charlie replied as calmly as if the campus were around the corner. I slumped in the front seat and felt I was back in the coliseum now fending off the lions of anxiety. It was three in the morning by the time we picked up Ron at university housing, packed his gear in the car's trunk, and settled him in the front seat. I dozed in the back while Charlie and Ron kibitzed all the way to Brooklyn. We were still on the highway at five thirty, but fast approaching the lane that turned off to Carroll Street.

"We'll have you home in no time," Charlie remarked picking up speed. In saying so, he failed to signal and nearly collided with a car that had the right of way. Luckily, a traffic light flashed red and halted both vehicles. Having stopped alongside, the driver of the second car rolled down his window. In the semi-darkness, it was clear his face was screwed up in anger. Ever open to conversation, Charlie rolled down the window and glanced out amiably. His friendly look further enraged the driver who yelled at the top of his voice, "Look where you're going, you stupid bastard."

With Franciscan sweetness Charlie replied, "I am not stupid," and drove off.

My contact with Charlie, who was personally committed to nonviolence, bolstered my anti-Vietnam protests. I was a regular visitor at the Catholic Worker and knew Dorothy Day; her uncompromising attitude against all war confirmed several of my students in their choice of CO status. This did not ingratiate me with either the school's headmaster or president. Because my commitment to the classroom had been wholehearted, I was approved for theology, the last step before finishing the Jesuit course and being ordained. Two incidents nearly disqualified me. They attest to my preference for independent judgment over docile obedience.

Rabbi Dreyfus of Union Temple had invited me to bring some of prep's students to his Sabbath service. I accompanied a group of ten to his temple twenty minutes away. Though I was not a priest, as a Jesuit scholastic in religious vows I was required to wear black suit and clerical collar whenever I ventured forth. To the members of the Jewish community who saw me that evening, I resembled a priest. They addressed me as "Father" to the amusement of my students. To them I was always "Mister" in Jesuit parlance.

The cantor's rich tenor voice and the rabbi's eloquent sermon on the evening's scripture made the service memorable. I watched my students listen with rapt attention. Without any advanced warning, the rabbi called me to the chancel, introduced me as Father Roccasalvo, and then asked if I would share with the congregation my thoughts on being at Union Temple.

I introduced myself with the words of Jacob's son in the closing chapter of Genesis: "I am Joseph, your brother." I described a childhood experience in which I attended Shabbat services at the Jewish vacation camp owned by one of my father's clients.

"There I learned my Hebrew prayers and still say Hebrew grace before meals. I feel perfectly at home here," and then added, "Pius XII has insisted we Christians are all 'spiritual' Semites." I made some further comments on the evening's scriptures and then closed with the word "Shalom."

I received sustained applause to the rabbi's satisfaction and my students' delight. The reaction of prep's president was otherwise. I had made the headlines in Union Temple's bulletin, and a copy was sent to New York's archdiocesan office which in turn informed my superior. Summoned to his office, I found myself before an irate Jesuit brandishing the block print. Temperamentally he was a caring man but gruff in his expression. As a former Korean chaplain who had seen action in the field, he was not to be bandied with. I remembered the gun in his desk drawer.

"Sit down," he said brusquely. He told me he had discussed my temple visit with the diocesan official responsible for religious affairs. I had gravely erred in ignoring the norms for ecumenical dialogue applicable only to the baptized. Jews did not qualify.

"Read this," he said, passing me the bulletin. I glanced at the words he had circled in red: "Father Roccasalvo"; "preaching"; "Prep students in attendance." I perceived a whiff of apprehension as I imagined wood being piled at the stake. I handed him the bulletin and apologized for any embarrassment.

"I did not mean to prevaricate," I said, using a word too nuanced for the situation.

"Who gave you permission?" he roared, banging his fist on his desk. "We're still figuring it out with the Protestants, and you're off on your own with the Jews. And you took students with you. Do you know the calls I got from parents upset at their sons being in a temple?"

"I didn't know."

"You're only a scholastic, not a priest, and you get up to preach. Who gave you permission?"

"Father," I replied, "I did not intend to misrepresent myself. It just happened. As for my students praying, they were responding to the evening's scripture which is also a part of our bible."

"But you preached," he said, pointing to the headline. "I want to know who gave you permission."

Standing up from my seat, I said to him, "Father, if you check the second chapter of St. Luke's Gospel, you will find Jesus also preached in the temple. There is precedent." I turned and walked out.

My candor resulted in the denial of drinks to the scholastics—a punishment meted out for my thoughtless behavior. Drinks were offered us at the day's end in the Father's rec room, and now we were forced to go dry. After two abstemious weeks, the beetle of the scholastics pressed me to apologize: "Your attitude is penalizing us." Meeting shortly after with the rector, I somehow made amends and drinks were restored.

The second incident proved more serious because of public exposure. It occurred during the visit of a prestigious alumnus who was a recently retired admiral. He had been invited to address the whole school about Jesuit education and its effects on his life. His was to be the "Without Them I Would Not Be Here" accolade presented by a graduate to his Jesuit hosts. And they were all in attendance on stage: the rector and headmaster;

the prefect of discipline and spiritual counselors; and foremost, the Jesuit provincial of secondary education, who visited prep to honor the admiral. The school auditorium was packed (as they say) to the rafters. After-school activities were suspended so that the student body could be present.

We filed into the gymnasium according to years. The senior classes and their homeroom teachers were closest to the stage. Since I was one of them, I sat on the aisle in the third row with the admiral clearly in view. He received warm applause after the flattering introduction by the rector, who touted the admiral for having been a brilliant tactician and a brave soldier in active combat. The admiral replied by saying that he "owed it all to the Jesuits."

His talk began innocuously enough as he recalled his prep years. But soon a shift in tone occurred as he enjoined the students to unquestioning obedience, "the hallmark of the Jesuit order." Without warning he launched into a tirade against those who challenged the government's involvement in Vietnam, since so many young men had lost their lives to keep the world free from communism.

"These protesters are traitors," he said, "and that also goes for the clerics on the picket lines."

My homeroom students, especially those in the Christian Action Core, shifted their posture in my direction to observe my reaction. The blood had left my face and my hands tingled from agitation. The admiral continued his rhetorical assault. During a pause in his talk, I stood up and left my seat. I walked up the aisle, in full view of the entire school, to the gym's front door, my back to the admiral and all on stage. During that infinite distance, I was trembling and thought my legs would buckle. There was not a sound in back of me except what resounded in my mind, the lyrics now more personalized: "I gotta get outa this place."

I left the school and hastened to the Brooklyn Botanic Garden to the peace enclave designed in Zen style. I sat on a bench while the tremors diminished, and I realized the enormity of what I had done. *It's over,* I thought, *How will I ever go back?*

When I did finally return for dinner, I was isolated in the dining room and left to eat at a table where no one sat. I had become the school's pariah as the rector and the headmaster each sidled up to excoriate me for my blatant rudeness to one of prep's own. The next day was Ash Wednesday, and as I waited in my classroom for the first period to begin, the loudspeaker came on. The headmaster apologized to the school for my singular discourtesy.

To my students I was a hero. Rebellion appears admirable to youth whenever a David confronts a Goliath. My action prompted discussion in the teachers' room, and several commended me on initiating dialogue about the war's morality. I took little comfort in their plaudits. I was left with disquietude about what would happen. It was the provincial for secondary education who took my part as I learned years later; he stood firm in his conviction that I be approved for theology. I can guess how the rector reacted: "A good teacher, yes, devoted to his students, no question. But he puts his own will first and bends superiors to it. He's not one of the troops."

I'm reminded of a similar judgment rendered years later during graduate teaching at Loyola University. I was invited to coffee by the provincial of the Chicago province. We knew each other well for we had lived together at John La Farge House in Cambridge, Massachussetts, a family home converted to meet the needs of Jesuits doing studies at Harvard. After finishing his PhD, Bob taught in a university, was made its president, and then was pulled from administration to become Jesuit provincial. His ascent up the hierarchy to that imposing position was easy to predict from both stature—he was over six feet tall—and voice which took its pitch from the lower register. He had the ability to boom out orders whenever necessary. His intelligence was matched by his prudence, and numerous were the times when he admonished me for an intemperate remark notable for humor but "way out of the ball park."

During the afternoon of our café appointment, I expected a similar admonition. He had heard that I had signed out of the Jesuits on Easter, the feast of the Resurrection, and was attuned to the action's implied symbolism. He wished to register disapproval in no uncertain terms. Jesuit provincials, being major superiors, were used to having the final word. Once our coffee had arrived, he got down to the business of making his point, no prefacing of remarks and no finessing of words, but a blunt appraisal:

"From what I've heard through the grapevine, you were on a collision course with your superior."

"Is that what it was?" I picked up the image and extended the metaphor. "As I recall, I wasn't speeding but driving cautiously within my own lane. The provincial was weaving in and out. He kept cutting me off."

"Provincials can't always leave their men alone. We'd like to, but surveillance is necessary."

"I find it demeaning to be monitored."

"Only if behavior warrants it. I gather you were off on your own. We've been instructed by Rome to pull people back to community. You took it on yourself to decide where you would live."

"Yes, but I was told repeatedly to find housing. For years I had permission. Suddenly a superior is installed who develops a moral squint and disapproves of my actions. I'm told I'm bending obedience to please myself."

"And how did you react?"

"By your norms, intemperately. I told the provincial I had taken three vows of poverty, chastity, and obedience. Infantilization was not one of them."

"Your superior, Joseph, was letting you know who was in charge. If you were one of my men, I would have done the same. I would have said you wanted more freedom than I could give."

"You know, Bob, I find that statement rather odd coming from someone schooled in scholastic philosophy."

"What do you mean?"

"You cannot give me freedom. I'm already free. Along with being rational, it's one of the qualities of my spiritual nature. What you're saying is that I take liberties with my freedom of which you don't approve."

I do not know how he answered. My own reply may have cornered him. Whatever my spiritual prerogatives, I may have denied him one of his: to have the last word.

I finished my first year of theology at Woodstock College, Maryland, before returning to New York; there, in two semesters and a summer, I completed the rest of my courses for the MDiv program. I was eager to clear the decks before beginning graduate studies. Age was an issue—I was soon to turn thirty-one—and I wasn't certain how long I would remain teachable. Languages like Sanskrit and Pali were needed to earn the PhD. The rigors of Indian grammar were sure to test my memory.

Canonical requirements for priesthood meant four years of theology. Jesuits who completed three were ordained and then added a fourth as newly minted priests. My swiftness in finishing in two posed a problem. What could the dean of studies do? I had an enviable grade point average. Though not required, I had taken intensive Hebrew at Union Theological with the formidable George Landis and received an A grade. I had every reason to make my case to the rector: I wanted to move out and be on my own for a year. He at first demurred and then agreed. I rented a tiny studio apartment on Park Avenue and Eighty-fourth Street where I resided with my Abyssinian cat, Octavian. Every day I walked to the Convent of the Sacred

Heart on Ninety-first Street and Fifth Street where I taught comparative religion to the first and fourth year girls in the upper school. I was happy to be away from theology; happy too not to be gagging on its scholasticism and triumphalism. I later satirized my two year theological stint in a short story called *Anathema,* in which Quentin Avery's misbegotten but funny language earns him condemnation from the Congregation for the Doctrine of the Faith. Like him I balked at Christian theology's inability to find an unassuming place among the world's religions. Religious events occurring outside the Christian faith found their validity by pointing to the Gospel. God seemed to be on sabbatical leave in the East until Jesus was born.

My interest in comparative religion dates to the time when I was completing my MA degree in English. A course in literary criticism required my reading one critic and determining why his theory helped to clarify literature. I chose Rabindranath Tagore. In 1913 he was the first Indian to have received the Nobel Prize for his English version of *Gitanjali,* his collection of mystical poems. W. B. Yeats praised them for their incomparable beauty; I was equally entranced. His theory that the artistic act springs from the abundance of the spirit impressed me. Like Gandhi who rose above religious separatism, he was broadly theistic in religious expression whether playing the novelist, essayist, or consummate short story writer. While reading his biography, I absorbed India's colorful myths and myriad doctrines, and found myself drawn to the Buddhist version. I was still ignorant about how to situate Christian theology in its global context. A Jesuit friend, appreciating my dilemma, suggested that I speak with Thomas Berry. He had initiated Fordham's doctoral program in the history of religions, which flourished for over a decade. In 1971, I met him on the Bronx campus.

As soon as I entered his office, I knew by observation I was in the right place. A blackboard behind his desk was covered with Chinese and Sanskrit words. I reacted favorably to the exotic visuals, but more so to the man who greeted me. His look combined benevolence with wisdom, and he quickly won me over by his compassionate listening. The smile on his face resembled Buddha's, but I was still quite far from making that connection. I introduced myself by telling him how I had received his name.

"And how can I help you?" he asked.

"Prof. Berry, I'm feeling trapped. I finished my theological requirements for Jesuit priesthood and I want to be ordained. But I need to know how all of it fits within the framework of world's religions. At the moment I think I'm signing up for propaganda. Theology gave me concentration, but I'm hungry for range."

"How did you come by this interest?"

"It began with a graduate paper on Tagore's literary theory. I read his poetry and it moved me. A Hindu's words had touched me as deeply as any Christian's. While reading his biography, I also felt drawn to the Buddhist sources."

"As a Jesuit you've done classical languages?"

"Ten years of Latin and nine of Greek. I recently finished an intensive course in biblical Hebrew."

Tom rose from his seat. I followed him as we left his office for the Fordham campus. I did not know where we were going until we arrived at the university bookstore. He found a shopping cart, and I followed him up and down the aisles as he reached for books. We walked over to a checkout counter, and the sales girl rang up a charge of over a hundred dollars. Tom paid with his credit card and then handed me a shopping bag.

"You'll find here all you need: grammars, dictionary, and texts. With your knowledge of classics, Sanskrit shouldn't come as a complete surprise."

"Sanskrit?"

"Yes. You'll need it before you begin any serious study of Indian religion. If you have difficulties, phone me after eleven."

"Don't you have classes?"

"I mean eleven at night. We can handle problems without interruption."

He left me with a smile informed by wry humor. Something pixilated in his manner charmed me. I was not accustomed to authority inviting so much liberty of choice. I thanked him warmly and we shook hands.

When I returned to my apartment, my cat Octavian was as eager as I to examine the shopping bag. I still have the books Tom bought me: Perry's *A Sanskrit Primer*; Macdonnell's *Sanskrit Grammar* and *A Practical Sanskrit Dictionary*; also, bilingual versions of the *Bhagavad Gita* and several *Upanishads*.

During lunch breaks while teaching at the Convent school, I took my primer to the Episcopal Church of the Heavenly Rest, sat in the Mary Chapel, and memorized Sanskrit paradigms. I could count on being the church's sole visitor. When in the following spring I had received Harvard's acceptance letter and the promise of scholarship aid, I prepped for the fall semester by reading the *Gita* with a Columbia student who was adept in Sanskrit, Persian, and Arabic. By the time I arrived in Cambridge in the fall of 1972, I was able to forego the Sanskrit requirement and begin the Pali language with Prof. Nagatomi. I had Tom to thank for his whimsical intervention at a bookstore, and for the nightly conversations that steered me through the intricacies of Sanskrit.

Thomas Berry was the mentor who directed me toward comparative religion, another precursor who made straight my path. Over the years I lost contact with him, but I heard his name bruited as the premier historian of cultures who now enhanced the relationship of humans to the cosmos. His sense of enchantment extended to his capricious title: he called himself a "geologian." His was another case of serious fun.

I have indicated how in residing in a studio at Eighty-fourth Street and Park I was accompanied by an Abyssinian cat called Octavian. His later presence during my Harvard studies was by special permission. How and why I received it is anecdotally rich and worth repeating.

In September 1972, I arrived early evening at the Center for the Study of World Religions to take up residence before starting my program in comparative religion. What was counted a year of theology became my first year of doctoral work. Books and clothes in cardboard boxes had preceded me, but I still arrived with both hands full: in my left was a garment bag and in my right, a cat-carrying case. John and Ineke Carman, who were expecting me, met me in the Center's lobby. There were warm greetings and a joint eagerness to show me to my digs, for they saw the traveler's strain on my face. I had been on the road for seven hours. My departure from Manhattan was aggravated by hellish traffic and an equally infernal heat wave. So I looked to get settled quickly in what the Center gave single students: an efficiency apartment. It was as compact as any New York studio, and at a third of the price, it was in New York parlance a terrific deal.

As I turned to climb the cement steps which led to the upper landing, Mrs. Carman noticed what was in my right hand.

"Is that a cat?" she asked with Dutch candor.

"Yes," I replied. "He's an Abyssinian. His name is Octavian."

"But Mr. Roccasalvo, animals aren't permitted at the Center."

Her remark startled me. I had read the instructions mailed me from the Center about moving in. Nothing in them forbade a cat. I made it known to Mrs. Carman and apologized for my ignorance of the Center's rules. I had not intended to flout them.

"You're correct about what you read," Dr. Carman said, "but we've never had a student arrive with a cat. We're sensitive to the religious needs of those who live here. Your cat can stay overnight, but I'm afraid you won't be able to keep him. Tomorrow morning you can speak with Prof. Smith in his office. I'll make an appointment for nine thirty."

So I trudged up the stairs to my apartment and freed Octavian from his carrying case. Before unpacking, I arranged a litter box, opened a can of tuna, and set out some water. With predictable curiosity Octavian inspected what he believed was his new home. Pleased by the room's simple arrangement, he committed it to feline memory, and then turned to enjoy a leisurely dinner. I went to bed and slept fitfully.

The next morning at nine thirty, I was sitting opposite Prof. Smith. At this first meeting with the Center's director it was odd to be discussing a cat.

"I'm sorry about the lapse in the instruction we mailed," he said. "In the future we will need to include a clause about animals. It's a question of ritual cleanliness."

"But are all animals unclean to religious people?" I asked, as if examining preliminarily a topic for a graduate paper. "Maybe cats are an exception."

"That's an enchanting question," Prof. Smith replied. "Perhaps you might want to research it and share your findings."

"I know that cats are allowed in Hindu and Buddhist temples because they're excellent mousers. But I don't know how Muslims view them."

"It appears you have your research cut out for you. I'm eager to hear what you learn. It might make a difference in the outcome," Prof. Smith added with characteristic openness.

I left his office wondering how and where I should begin. I walked over to Widener Library, hoping to find a special listing on cats and comparative religion. I pored through the card catalog, fruitlessly checking books in C Southwest, and came away learning a lot about monkeys in the *Mahabharata*. It wasn't until I mentioned my frustration to a friend who was majoring in Islamic studies that I received any help.

"You might phone Prof. Annemarie Schimmel who's currently at Harvard. She's a renowned Islamic scholar whose specialty is Sufism. I recall seeing a picture in her office of the sacred cat of Egypt, the one from the Met collection."

"Octavian is of the same lineage. It's in the face and the torso. He even has the same whippet tail."

He gave me Prof. Schimmel's number at the university. I was in luck and reached her on the first try. I explained who I was and Octavian's plight. She listened sympathetically.

"I think I can help you," she said with confidence. "I'll leave an envelope with the Center's secretary. You'll have it tomorrow."

The next morning, as promised, a manila envelope awaited me. Within I found a Persian miniature of the Prophet sitting with the Qur'an open on his lap. Asleep in his turban was a cat. Underneath, in elegant Arabic script, Prof. Schimmel had cited a hadith, the treasured tradition that expressed Muhammad's verbal approval. She had translated for my benefit: "Love of cats is part of the faith."

I presented my evidence to Prof. Smith and learned shortly after that Octavian could stay. Henceforth, cats were permitted at the Center, a fact attested to by Bill Graham's two long-haired cats of uncertain parentage, Wellington and Winnifred, who arrived later. Meanwhile, I was often seen with Octavian whom I kept on a leash as he prowled the Center's courtyard.

"What a beautiful cat," my next-door Muslim neighbor said on seeing him for the first time.

"Yes," I answered. "He's our resident Coptic Christian."

Octavian lived with me at Apley Court during my years as tutor for Dudley House, and it was there he died of uremia. Here is my poem eulogizing him as published in *101 Favorite Cat Poems:*

Homage to Octavian

Who said cats have nine lives has told untruth.
For I once shared four lives with such a one
That bounded up the heights of feline youth
And, at the summit, shone so like the sun,
His angles were like angels. Yet undone
Was he, for though a cat of high estate,
He chose, in the fifth year of reign, to abdicate.

I wonder how Egypt, then, could bend its knee
And magnify his name as lord and liege,
And bow to all his elusive majesty,
Intoning words meant solely to besiege
That high-born soul to show noblesse oblige.
For he was to the godhead next of kin
Being, at all times, all he could have been.

But as for me, it was always otherwise;
I never knelt before his sinuous grace
Nor made obeisance to those lustrous eyes.
I lived too close to miracles to embrace
Him more than as a splendid commonplace.
And though he seemed to the gods their next of kin,
He proved to be mortally beautiful: Octavian.

Years before his death, when he was vitally beautiful, Octavian had
watched me apply to graduate school in the tiny Park Avenue apartment
which he shared with me. It was also there that I prepared for my final
exam in all of philosophy and theology called the *ad gradum*. I earned

the grade of ten for the two hour oral and received my master of divinity degree *summa cum laude*. In the middle of this intellectual ferment, I never stopped trying to be contemplative whether at prayer, during liturgy, or in the classroom. I've since come to believe that without a special grace, what Christian mysticism calls *gratia gratis data*, it is virtually impossible to keep an inner peace in a tumultuous world. The Trappist abbot of Genesee was accurate when he called Jesuits presumptuous for engaging in humanistic pursuits without mystical accompaniment. "Instead of finding God in all things," he remarked, "some Jesuits just find things." He admitted the gallant attempt at trucking up to the natural world and dealing with it on its terms. Without a supernatural sense, one entered through its door and never came out one's own.

I'm frequently taken for an SJ. Is it the spaciousness of Jesuit thought which I share and the zest for rescuing reverence by irony? Or is it the arduous effort to think with the church and then achieve only damage control?

Novitiate meant to prepare me for an active ministry. But it drew on monastic means to accomplish it. So effective was the monkish isolation in compromising the goal of apostolic service that I nearly left to join the Carthusian order in Vermont. Silence and solitude made me hungry to secure an atmosphere conducive to the prayer of quiet. I offer here an emended version given by Robert Hugh Benson:

> I begin by an act of self-exclusion from the world of sense. I
> force myself inward and downward till the kneeler, the crucifix,
> the room all seem apart, and I am left a solitary, too languid
> to stir. I make my second descent, renouncing all I possess,
> my mind and heart aware of the Presence in which they find
> themselves; they cling close to the will, their lord and protector.
> The Presence surges about me as I sink to that peace which

follows relinquishment of thought, and there I rest. Above me there sounds the restless world, but I appear as though asleep. Beyond sense and reflection, in that place to which I have learned the road, in that region where my perceptions go with the swiftness of light; where truth is handled, known, and tasted, God Transcendent is now God immanent, and the divine mysteries are seen in a luminous darkness.

I have here compressed more than fifteen years in what would have taken volumes. Brevity heightens my choices in the pointillism of events. If you step back, the splashes of biography may produce coherence. These memories are my palette. While attached to them, I anticipate their final disappearance; they are residues of an obsolete way of life. Any effort to secure them in time will never succeed.

ix

I was fortunate to share the visionary community of Harvard's Center for the Study of World Religions. I had enrolled in the doctoral program known as Field I. I already had the requirements for comparative research since I was versed in one tradition, the Judeo-Christian, along with its attendant languages: ten years of Latin, nine of Greek, and two of biblical Hebrew. For comparison I chose as my second tradition Indian Pali Buddhism (Theravada) which forms the religious basis for the five South Asian countries known collectively as Southern Buddhism. I give here the time-honored names: Ceylon, Burma, Cambodia, Laos, and Thailand. The language of their shared Buddhist scriptures, Pali, is Indo-European and cognate to Latin and Greek. Pali's bewildering inflections came as no surprise since I had been schooled at Brooklyn Prep in inflected languages. Sanskrit which multiplied these inflections with a vengeance was another matter but still no surprise.

Jesuit graduate students were reputed to be at an advantage. It was said that their religious affiliation constituted a third tradition that proved another resource. Jesuits too brought with them prior degrees. Mine after college were an MA in English literature, a Licentiate in Philosophy, and an MDiv in theology. Harvard loved us Jesuits. Like good Jewish boys at the local yeshiva, we had done our homework. Harvard would empower us to accomplish what we could not do on our own. But Jesuits were also desirable candidates because the celibacy we professed simplified our emotional lives and enabled us to focus on our studies with almost marital fervor. It was true. Living at Harvard's Center in that austere efficiency apartment, surrounded by graduate students equally bent on the doctorate was like reentering a second novitiate. I was used to the formal demands of papers and exams, and I could sit through the rigors of translating page after page of Pali Buddhist texts. I took three years of the language and worked with it for another three while doing my doctoral research and writing my thesis. I think there were times when my dreams were in Pali with no required subtitles. In my first year I logged in over six hundred hours. With two other students I sat in a cubicle in the basement of Yen Ching Library. I was the only one formally registered for Indian Studies 120a and 120b. My mentor was Masatoshi Nagatomi, a one-man show; he knew all the major languages of Buddhism: Chinese, Japanese, Pali, Tibetan, and Buddhist Hybrid Sanskrit. His desk was precariously piled with books, manuscripts, global correspondence, and doctoral dissertations. He found at a glance in any of his canons of Buddhist scripture the arcane passage he was seeking, and he translated it at sight while offering a fluent explanation. Sometimes his English faltered in deciding the word that best caught the Buddhist nuance. He often turned to me to supply it. A man of prodigious Buddhist lore, the memory of him still inspires me, for he graciously but firmly brought me through the doctoral process by setting feasible goals for my comprehensives, for thesis chapters, and for my doctoral defense. He also encouraged me to proceed with priestly ordination.

Born in 1926 in western Japan, he was the eldest son and presumed successor priest to the family Buddhist temple belonging to the Jodo Shinshu sect. He traveled the country as a young man accompanied by Buddhist priests, his father and grandfather. He learned the sutras in preparation for the day when he would succeed them as head of the family's temple. It never happened. Recognized as a gifted student, Mas went to Harvard where he received his PhD in 1957, and then remained as instructor of Sanskrit. In 1969 he was named Harvard's first professor of Buddhist Studies, and maintained that title for thirty-eight years.

I think Mas saw in my priesthood something to which he had also aspired but left undone. In a substitutive way I would complete what he never finished. He said to me one day as we took a break from translation:

"You know, Joe, I would honor your decision if you did not get ordained. I would respect you more if you did."

"Why, Prof. Nagatomi?"

"It's because you have a gift for translation. Your Catholic background helps you understand Buddhist text and context. As a priest, you would be a valuable bridge between Buddhism and Christianity. Of course you could do that without being ordained. But being a priest would ensure a greater impact."

Only once in my academic dealings was I ever at odds with him. It happened on Holy Thursday. We had spent two hours translating the Pali of the *Paranibbana Sutta* which describes the Buddha's passage into nirvana. Nagatomi's impromptu comments had so interrupted my translating that we never finished the text.

"Oh, Joe, let's finish this tomorrow before I give you another assignment."

"Prof. Nagatomi, I won't be here," I replied without explaining myself.

"And why is that?" he added with a curiosity bordering on sternness. Mas had a zest for translation. Preferring the solitary encounter with a student to holding forth in a crowded lecture hall, he was reluctant to miss an opportunity.

"It's Good Friday," I replied. "Out of respect for the day, I'll be absent from all my classes."

"Yes, of course," he said and then added. "May I offer a respectful comment? We Buddhists are used to seeing the wayside Buddha seated tranquilly in lotus position with his eyes averted and his awareness lost in enlightenment. It is a figure of serenity and reminds us that if he preached suffering, he also preached the end of it. His statue is an assurance that what he experienced may also be ours. So it's only with difficulty that I look on the figure of the crucified Christ. It is an image of relentless pain and a terrible sight. Contrasted with the Buddha's peace it is shocking, and I have to turn my eyes away. Yet the cross is the central image of Christianity. It's a great stumbling block for us Buddhists. Perhaps you could help me here."

"The problem, Prof. Nagatomi, if I may be frank, is that you see the cross that you see, but you don't see the cross that I see. To me it's not just a symbol of pain but a sign of divine compassion and of costly love. Finally, it's an image of redemptive suffering."

I do not recall his response, but I do know he cancelled his Good Friday's classes out of respect for his Christian students. It was not until Easter Monday after having celebrated Christ's Resurrection that we again met in class and read about the Buddha's ascent into nirvana. It proved a congenial match of events.

The years of living at the Center were followed by my residence as a Harvard tutor under the leadership of Jean Mayer, an international expert in nutrition. There I came into contact with brilliant pedagogues of every stripe. What they all shared was a broad humanism. They were also the best in their sphere of competence; in short, they were outstanding. Within this class of luminaries Wilfred Cantwell Smith, *emeritus* professor, historian of Islam, and comparative religious expert, shone with a special radiance. It was he who directed our studies during an era best described as the

Center's Periclean age. His devotion to his students was legendary, and it was not unusual for him to return an essay of twenty-five pages with nine of his own in which he reacted, paragraph by paragraph, to the originating text. Every word was appraised for its import, and such high seriousness sparked in the writer the urge to go and do likewise. Four years after his retirement from Harvard, when I decided to divide my time between teaching and writing fiction, I visited him in Halifax and received his academic blessing.

"What you are essaying to do, Joe, if I grasp your intent, is definitely of Harvard," he remarked in his studied diction. Only he could have said "of Harvard" as if he were translating the Latin, *Harvardiani*. I could still see chapter and page of Henle's *Latin Grammar* explaining the descriptive genitive; how its use was obligatory in phrases of worth, rank, value, and kind.

It was not until December 1988 that I sent him my third novel, *Chartreuse*; it prompted a written endorsement that what I was "essaying" was clearly "of Harvard." The novel arrived during a painful period when Wilfred was hospitalized. I share the letter here. It is still a source of pride and encouragement:

> Dear Joe:
>
> It turns out that a total hip replacement, though something that in the long run can be successful and a welcome delight, at first is not fun; the fortnight that I spent in the hospital following it proved less than delightful. (I have been home now for a couple of days, and with that I am delighted, even though recovery will continue slowly.) Nonetheless, I discovered in hospital the best possible way to outwit the post-operative problems; I might almost say, the only possible way, except that the matter is at the moment available to a lucky few. It is:

to read a rich, engaging, exciting, intelligent, gripping novel, written by a friend of mine—about the part of France that I love best, about people with whom one can immediately identify or sympathize, or about whom one comes quickly to care . . . I could go on and on. In other words, I not merely enjoyed *Chartreuse*; I loved it. My congratulations are vigorous. My thanks to you for sending it are warm and deep—to say nothing of my thanks to you for writing it.

This note must be brief: I am still quite weak. Let me wish you, on behalf of both Mrs. Smith and myself, a joyous and deep Christmas. And more power to your pen!

Sincerely yours,
Wilfred Cantwell Smith

In a second letter written years later after reading my short stories, Wilfred thanked me again: "I told you when you sent the Chartreuse story how much I admire people who can write literary and not merely academic things, and I certainly hope that you will continue along this not merely pleasant but important line."

I continue to act on that sentiment which was my first endorsement from a *litterateur*. Smith was my stamp of approval.

During my fourth year of studies, I was slated to be ordained a priest, a goal for which I had "trained" over a decade. I mentioned earlier how psychiatric intervention helped me clarify my issues. What finally induced me to proceed were my comparative studies at Harvard and the contacts the university engendered with Masatoshi Nagatomi and Wilfred Smith. To explain myself better, I will transcribe a letter to Daniel Conlin, a priest friend and confidante. At the time, he was on the verge of ordination. Unable to attend, I chose to be present on paper; to share with him what the priesthood meant to me, and why I still saw it as a providential match of temperament. I have rarely been so transparent in print. But this memoir makes claims on my candor, and so I reproduce the letter here. Its tone oscillates between serious and playful, fervent and facetious. I'm a little on guard against my heart, and cautious too that my mind should remain in the lead. I'm not surprised. I'm wary of excess in writing prose, and the attitude extends to religious enthusiasm.

June 2, 1990

Dear Dan:

It disappointed me to inform your family that I would not be present for your Ordination Day and the festivities after. This letter is one way to be with you, and to reinforce a friendship which I've come to value deeply. Since a shared vocation now brings us closer, I chose to set down reflections about my own priesthood embraced fifteen years ago. In the interim, I have resented and balked at it, been awed and overwhelmed by it, but never—how rarely I say never—have I regretted it. The finger of God is here, and in my case, surely all ten of them. For I put off the priesthood at least twice and had a terror of its rigors. In the end, it was my Cambridge group of agnostic friends, overt atheists, sexual athletes, lapsed Catholics, and Buddhist practitioners who urged me to get ordained. They seemed to say in unison, "If you can do this—and we're your friends—you will be a bridge to a church that appears closed to us. Our lives won't change that much, but our attitudes may. With you there, who knows what will happen? Anyway, you have a talent for it. So do it."

And *it* has proven to be an adventure: from kowtowing during Thai Mass to writing novels as parables of grace. Where else the Innovative One takes me I can't say, but this much is clear. As Blaise says in my novel, *Chartreuse,* "I can't be let go of." His words acknowledge a Providence that accounts for the stories I write, the places I visit, and the people with whom I consort. My intent is not obvious. Befriend them for their own good; become indispensable, and *en passant*, let them learn of the sacramental mark. Then allow them to cope with the surprise and walk away if it proves too much.

The context of discovery is irrelevant: from bars to bar bells, from park benches to cafés, it doesn't matter. The dress code too varies wildly: a clerical collar, blue jeans, a tux. But like the Messianic secret in Mark's gospel, the truth will out, and those to whom it comes must re-interpret all of what went before. They resemble the two disciples at Emmaus for whom Jesus breaks bread and, literally, gives himself away. If the apostles caught the gist of his divinity, it was by means of his heightened humanity. Even after the resurrection, his divine nature remained opaque until the Spirit's fiery descent. The disciples needed fifty days. Given their lack of mental agility, nothing would have benefited them less than a Pentecost that arrived too soon.

Something of the cloak and dagger appeals to my novelist's bent: the shifty saboteur; the Jesuit in false whiskers; the polyglot double agent; the spy in bath towel working the Turkish sauna. It can be amusing, poignant, even playful, but I don't mistake means for ends. If I'm at all effective, it's because I've been superseded. As the Zen Master says, "Be a finger pointing to the moon." But remember it's the moon that counts. Like the Baptist in Renaissance paintings, point to the Lamb of God and then disappear.

Preaching is the core of my priesthood. The rule is fixed: rarely keep a sermon. The temptation to remove an old one from the files is too tempting. It's better not to have it around. So I toss my notes after leaving the pulpit. Starting at zero keeps preaching fresh for zero is not nothing. It's perfect receptivity. I've never heard you preach as a deacon. No doubt it is done with conviction. I hope that you're unbudgeable like Luther and orthodox like Bellarmine, and that your suavity seeps through. As for complacency, you know too much about yourself to show any. Here an anecdote strikes a cautionary note. Once Father Berrigan asked me how my Sunday sermon went. I answered, "Successfully, I think, judging from the response." "Really," he replied, "How many walked out?" I leave it to you whether to imitate or admire him.

I'm always depleted after presiding at Mass. It's not the hours of preparation: checking texts, pursuing references, or reading commentaries. Nor is it the effort to integrate something literary. This past Sunday, for example, I cited Salinger's *Catcher in the Rye* in order to finish with a flourish. Still, for all the smiles I receive that I got the sermon right, I return home a vacuum. I immediately go to the gym to realign body with spirit. Inspiration followed by perspiration reconnects me, and in the absence of physical intimacy, working out is a godsend. Intimacy: now there's a word I could rehearse with you. It generates the fission between passion and celibacy, piety and worldliness, mysticism and realism. It's an unnerving mix. I watch the balancing act and gasp when I add another chair or stool; or when circling the rings round both arms, I maneuver the unicycle backward, hoping I won't plummet headlong without any net to break the fall.

For all the high jinks, I think you think I'm too porous to people. It's a fair assumption since I take a Mediterranean approach to the body. I'm more relaxed than guarded. The Manichean mistrust I observe in your rueful grin is not my manner. I don't believe in frisking at the sexual border; just occasional check points to allow for an easy passage.

About male and female in marriage, I'm too aware of complementarity in world religions to be casual. But experience tells me the ideal isn't always possible and asymmetry rules. People are fractured saints who hobble along. Loving where they can (and not where they can't) they often squeak through at the end before the door is bolted. While I value your prudence, justice and fortitude, try a dash of temperance so that all the moral virtues may spice your orthodoxy.

It's fitting to end this letter with poetry. I cite from memory Gerard Manley Hopkins' "The Habit of Perfection":

> O full-of-primrose hands, O feet
> That want the feel of plushy sward;
> And you shall walk the golden street
> And you unhouse (and house) the Lord.

Daniel, you have my heart-felt congratulations. You've traveled a tortuous road sometimes strewn with rocks, sometimes with boulders. You're familiar with rubble. With the resurrection stone rolled back, you managed to slip through unscathed and have arrived at your goal. In this year of Our Lord, 1990, I marvel at your embrace of priesthood. It emboldens me to another fifteen. My warmest regards,

Joseph

X

During my stay in Bangkok in 1975, I lectured in comparative religion at Mahidol University, researched my doctoral thesis, and said Mass for two religious communities. I resided with the Jesuits at Xavier Hall, Victory Monument, and from there I wrote my letters home. All have the same Thai letterhead, all were models of discretion. The tone throughout was lighthearted as I wrote of a difficult situation by putting my best spin on it. From a position of hindsight, three decades later, I realize these letters, while easing parental anxiety, were lacking in candor. In fact, they were an exercise in discretion. As narratives, they were substantially true. But close friends who chanced to read them—for my parents shared the exploits of their globe-trotting son—were not misled by my whimsical tone. Several wrote and asked me what was *really* going on. I kept my replies and for the sake of this memoir have conflated them into a single account.

My friends had read my letters and despite their murkiness dredged them for meaning. They challenged the maxim that the suppression of truth does not entail the expression of falsehood. They agreed with Horace when he wrote: *"Quod est verum, lateat quamvis, aliquando patebit"* (What is true, though it may lie concealed, will eventually be disclosed). Their difference with the poet was that they were unwilling to wait. They wanted the facts now without omission.

I explained that I was censuring my feelings in order not to alarm my family. I had left my father seriously ill but in remission from cancer. With her hyperactive mind, my mother was capable of imagining the worst: that her son would be harmed at a prohibitive distance. So I rarely spoke my mind on paper without finessing the truth. Everything was filtered through the fine mesh of happiness. I learned to be a fiction writer by reshaping my experience to meet the purpose of sounding content.

When I did write candidly to my friends, what did I say? My letters outlined the basics. For three hours every Monday I taught seven students who were pursuing an MA degree in comparative religion. It was the first time a South Asian university had launched a graduate program in which Buddhist students examined religions other than their own. The teaching proved difficult; the problem, one of understanding. Though I knew the material well, I was challenged to find points of contact between my students' Buddhist experience and concepts alien to it. How was I to explain the genius of biblical monotheism when Buddhism had no word for God? How should I deal with immortality in Egyptian religion when Buddhists rejected anything resembling the soul? How did one describe cosmic creation when Buddhism dismissed the idea as speculation? Buddhist pragmatism, apparent at every turn, summed up briskly the only two questions that mattered: Why do we suffer? How can it be stopped?

Operative in Thai culture was an attitude daunting to westerners and epitomized in the words, *mai pen rai*. This expression—and it's just an approximation—was rendered: "It doesn't matter." You heard it in conversation when things went awry, when they "didn't pan out." "Why be surprised at the result?" it asked. "It's in the nature of things. Nothing is reliable for reality changes from moment to moment. It's not the status quo but the *fluxus quo*."

Mai pen rai challenged the judgment that solid means produce definite ends. It was galling to Americans intent on getting things done. I was one of them. For five years I had pored over Buddhist texts which insisted that all entities, whether persons, places, or things, were *anicca*: without any underlying permanence. To treat them otherwise was to invite suffering. Despite daily exposure, I had not internalized the truth that "the center will not hold" (Yeats).

My novel, *Fire in a Windless Place*, addresses this attitude in a conversation between the female protagonist, Maia Ratanakorn, and her former lover, Dr. David McCauley:

> "You know that Thai phrase we use, *mai pen rai*? It's translated 'never mind.' It's a decent rendition. You arrive late for a dinner party or you forget to come. Your host answers your apology with *mai pen rai*: 'Don't get upset, it doesn't matter.' It points to a Thai attitude. It expresses this country's Buddhism, a shrugging off of impermanence. To an exacting mind like yours, David, I imagine it's exasperating. But it's basic to my life. I'm no longer flattened by disappointment. I've gone back to my roots and become casual. I've learned to prefer laughter to tears."

I was not as flexible as Maia. Thai preference for loose commitments together with the heat and humidity wore me out and made each day a struggle: from standing in a packed bus to maneuvering in the crowded streets. I scarcely kept my balance while Bangkok's residents remained unflappable, always smiling, always composed, with an inquisitive stare that caught the strain in my face. "Why so intense?" they seemed to ask. "We Buddhists live at a much cooler temperature. *Mai pen rai.*" Gradually I learned that this attitude wasn't fatalistic, but sprang from a protean awareness that saw each situation as new. I marveled at their emotional neutrality, how Thais smiled during traffic jams made worse by torrential rain. Exceptions to the equanimity were the Jesuit missionaries who entered the rec room at day's end and collapsed from fatigue. Whatever their success, it vanished by morning. Plans had to be scuttled because of student absenteeism, and the Jesuits started over from scratch.

Spoken Thai was another challenge. I had five hours of class a week whose sole purpose was to help me move unescorted around the city. Since Thailand was never colonized, I could not use French as I might have in Vietnam. English was spoken by a small number in diplomatic or hotel service. So learning Thai was *de rigueur*. I applied myself studiously but the pitfalls were many. The five tones of low, middle, high, rising, and falling were readily mastered along with Thai syntax. But the slightest shift in voice produced ambiguity and a shrug of the shoulders as the listener walked away. The unwitting error and its social consequence heightened the embarrassment. I offer a memorable example.

On the first Sunday after my arrival, I was asked to assist at Mass by distributing the Eucharist. In preparation I was given the Thai words for "the body of Christ," but in the sanctuary nerves became my undoing. By the time I appeared on the altar, my tones had dropped. The result was humorous but no communicant laughed. After Mass while sitting at breakfast with the Jesuits, I repeated myself to their amusement.

"You mean I got it wrong?"

"Yes."

"What was I distributing?"

"Fried chicken."

It was a poor debut for which nothing could have prepared me.

Twice weekly I said Mass for the Brothers of St. Gabriel, a religious community that taught young Buddhists. To accommodate their schedule, I was up at five fifteen and out on the street by five forty. While waiting for bus 54 in the eerie morning light, I watched the saffron-clad monks processing in single line with begging bowls. In my mind's eye, I saw the Buddhist texts providing me with commentary.

The Philippine brothers were committed but overworked. Drifting through liturgy like sleepwalkers, they attended Mass in pre-Vatican II manner as passive spectators. Since I knew neither Tagalog nor Thai, I preached in neither language. Forced to use English in explaining scripture, I dispensed with combining humor and gravity, and thus sacrificed satisfaction with this otherwise admirable group. At Xavier Hall I refused to say daily Mass with no one in attendance as if it were a closet drama. Liturgy offered me something prayerful when an English-speaking priest arrived with whom I concelebrated. Apart from that, it was a liturgical desert.

The Jesuits were a remarkably zealous group; it comprised an Austrian, an Italian, two Spaniards, and an American who spent weeks away in preached retreats to religious brothers or sisters. But zeal is rarely diverting. Conversation at meals flagged, and the repartee with amusing companions was entirely lacking. Perhaps their common vocation could not surmount the national differences. Whatever the reason, the emotional vacuum came as a shock. I pined for the friendships I had made in Cambridge. Times were when I felt so depleted that I had no reserves for research. I sought out foreign visitors who enlivened the atmosphere. Refugee priests from Laos, Burma, and Vietnam came to Xavier Hall in a steady stream. I was grateful for their varied presence even if meals sounded like Babel revisited. I once counted seven nationalities with their respective languages. The Italian superior occasionally attended to my western needs. He had the workmen install a powerful air-conditioner in the transom above my bedroom door, and for the first time in weeks I slept a full night. The hum of the unit obliterated the incessant noise from Victory Monument. His was a kind gesture and it came from one who stinted on money.

I resented how the Jesuits poured their energies into their work to the detriment of communal sharing. But it freed my resourcefulness in making friends with whom I fraternized: an Ursuline Sister who liked bars; an Indonesian grad student with a taste for pizza and movies; a student activist from the October Revolution who frequented beer halls; a Jesuit scholastic with a penchant for ballet and boogying. So my companions went. I left with them on weekends and returned to the community Mondays with the look of having swallowed the local canary.

Friends served another purpose; they were a defense against indiscretion. Sexual connection came easily in Bangkok with men or women. Preferences ran in both directions, and the beguiling culture accepted any, alone or in combination. At night I never ventured out alone. The local joy boys and bar girls approached and tugged at your arm, trying to erode your resolve. And if willpower hovered on the brink, memory reminded you of the venereal disease rampant in the city. Still, it took discipline to thwart the ubiquitous pleasures. The danger passed with the simple distractions of writing letters, seeing a film, or engaging in sports at the local health club.

My friends weighed the evidence and their verdict was unanimous. I was not happy. True, I kept despondency at bay because I had a clear goal. My letters were no protracted SOS. But my Asian sojourn taught me about temperament: I could tolerate a charmless room, a tasteless diet, and a rigorous schedule. But I could not survive without depth in relationships. Without it I was irascible and my humor transmogrified into sarcasm. My situation was as good as it gets for I lived close to the university where I taught. I now had an air-conditioned bedroom and office, and I could summon bilingual secretaries to help with translation. I had a safe address, and food and water I trusted; in short, all the basics for secure habitation in an exotic corner of the world. None of it sufficed. With black ink I ploughed through the days until the time I was slated to return home.

Lunch and dinner out, trips at short notice, an entourage of persons with whom to chum around: all of it eased my solitude and allowed me to push on with research. Thus I completed all my interviews and had almost two hundred pages of dialogue. I succeeded in reaching my quota of twenty-five Thai professionals who included prestigious monks, professors, and psychiatrists. I stumbled on this last group who had aligned psychoanalysis with Buddhist doctrine. I later published my findings in an article on Thai Buddhist psychiatry.

It was a prodigious effort to make these contacts. Harvard had not prepared me to be a sociologist of religion and an anthropologist. I learned quickly. I dashed about the city on a motorbike with my tape recorder slung over one shoulder. I moved from temple to campus to jungle in search of my sources. The result was a mixed narrative ranging from mystical abbots and innovative therapists to former monks and devout Buddhist professors. What emerged was a study of novelty and orthodoxy, contrast and affinity; in short, a Buddhist tradition and its vicissitudes. The juxtaposition of text and context pleased my Harvard mentor and doctoral readers who so concurred that I earned my PhD with honors. The award ceremony was a year and a half off. For the time being I stayed in Bangkok coordinating roles as lecturer, priest, research scholar, and language student. Any of these was taxing enough during the monsoon when wading through ankle-deep water was the sole transport from one city block to the next.

I fictionalized my Asian experience in *Fire in a Windless Place*. I prefer the novel to my dissertation which I now find ponderous. Still, without it I might not have imagined a literary version; more importantly, I would never have admitted to becoming Buddhist. What happened was a question of temperament. In Buddhism I felt I had come home.

After defending my dissertation, I took a postdoctoral course at the Boston Psychoanalytic Institute. There I attended a seminar on psychoanalysis and the human sciences. The participants were asked to connect their former doctoral work with depth psychology, and expose the difficulties if no connection seemed possible. Since my topic was the Buddhist denial of self, I had a heyday in addressing the seminar's purpose. Why, I asked, was Buddhist nirvana not psychosis? How did one square self denial with the ego viewed by psychoanalysis as a sign of mental health? Was Buddhist enlightenment "a temple of serenity built over a hole in space" as D. H. Lawrence said?

During the seminar, I learned how psychoanalytic freedom from compulsion strengthened the ability to choose and assured the equilibrium of the functioning ego. But taking refuge in the determinism of a fixed identity was still a possibility. The chance still existed of reaching a dead end by bowing to the storehouse of memory; of saying: "This past is mine. I am this past. This is my history. It's with me as having-been." The leopard was defending his permanent spots. No matter how deftly psychoanalysis exhumed the unconscious mind, past events could still be agents in setting the limits of the present. With its unbroken chain of cause and effect, the law of karma prevailed.

Buddhism offered a version of freedom called liberation. Because it denied a fixed identity in time and space, there was no self to be defended and no self to be offended. By reducing the self to flashes of experience, emotional life was freed from possessiveness and the unbudgeable past seen for what it was: a projection of "my" and "mine." Personhood as a rigid ordering of experience was trivialized, and with it, the autonomous self. What emerged was release from neurotic clinging. No longer came the invocation, "That's the way I am." Meditation became an exercise of letting go: not "I feel pain," but "this is a painful feeling"; not "I feel joy," but "this is a joyful feeling." Energy no longer moved toward the central ego but outward to the community.

The consequences for dealing with God and the world have proved invaluable. Concerning God—*when I'm thinking buddhistically*—I have let go of the word. God-talk becomes provisional and a form of conventional truth. It's a temporary idolatry I use and then dismiss in favor of the God beyond the god of orthodox theology. Here Iris Murdoch's witty dialogue in *The Good Apprentice* helps:

> "Perhaps just the word bothers me, the name, like 'God,' it's got so—" "Messy. Messed up. Like your image of falling into the hands of God—oh, I know you didn't mean *him*—but it's a deep place, an ocean heaving and giving birth to itself, melting and seething in itself and into itself, interpenetrating itself, light in light and light into light, swelling inwardly, flooding itself, part interpenetrating the rest until it spills and boils over."
> "What's that, sex, the unconscious?"
> "A description of God by a Christian mystic."
> "He must have been a heretic."
> "He was. All the best are."

Concerning the world, I realize it is not inhospitable, I am. The world is not askew, my mind is. Peace enjoins attunement to the way things are.

It means an astringent spirituality: of never saying more than you mean and never meaning more than you say; of living fully in the present but not for the present. In a world of change, *always* and *never* are inflexible. What's preferable is not yes or no but "nyes".

Concerning others, I remind myself that they are as mutable as I and just as vulnerable. Fragility value is transience value in time. Born of tenderness, the knowledge creates compassion and a genial irony. The conclusions are obvious: no romantic fervor about persons, places, or things but life at a cooler temperature. Intensity of attention, yes, but sensationalism and exaggeration—what the world calls "the big splash"—are to be shunned. They represent the mendacity of magnitude. Fireworks do not feed the aura of enlightenment, which comes suddenly but not quickly. Often I remind myself: "Be patient, Joseph. Paradise takes time."

Concerning my "self"—and the empirical reality remains—there is disinterested caring and no preoccupation with death; no search for happiness but a turning toward what gives equanimity. I have banished the word "permanence" from my vocabulary in exchange for "constancy." I'm no longer swept off my feet nor do I wait in the wings till I'm noticed. While I may be irreplaceable, I'm eminently substitutable. Having taken Auden's advice to heart, I look for "ironic points of light wherever the just exchange their messages." If psychoanalysis has bolstered my Buddhism, it resides in the insight that absolutizing persons, places, or things is to engage in infantilism. The only reality one may speak of absolutely is the Absolute.

As for Jesus, in the dereliction of the cross, his ego was reduced to zero by ordinary standards of selfhood. In a state of complete receptivity his "I" was crossed out and allowed humanity in. Because he was emptied of boundaries, he became "the works." Iris Murdoch adds that he is "our nondegradable love object and our local name for God."

I have a laminated picture on my bookshelf in which half the Buddha's face and half of Christ's merge in a unity. It's my preeminent icon, a picture of convergence. In my dual roles as priest and instructor of Buddhism, I engage in a shuttle diplomacy. The passage back and forth is exhilarating. Fortunately, I like to fly. But if ever I need to circle because of turbulence, when I finally land I coast to my appointed terminal, "Roman Catholicism."

"I doubt if you'd stay very long," said a friend versed in comparative religion. "You're more like a roaming Catholic."

"Your humor points to a truth," I replied. "Something itinerant resides in the Greek word *katholikos* which is a mark of the church. Being 'universal' means facing toward everything; it's a summons to spread the Gospel. And so Christian faith made the bumpy ride through the classical world. It sprouted in Jerusalem but traveled to Italian soil where it ripened and was harvested. Rome became home. Still, it's not why I stay a Catholic."

"Why then?"

"I like paradox. I pay attention when doctrines stab at each other in apparent contradiction like God is three yet one or Christ is human yet divine. Other antinomies keep me on red alert: nature and grace; scripture and tradition; faith and works; papal authority and freedom of conscience. They all proceed by the complementary dualism of both/and, but on the level of experience they feel like either/or. I find heresy which smoothes the inconsistencies rather boring. I prefer the adventure of orthodoxy."

"It sounds like G. K. Chesterton."

"He's my inspiration. He compares Christianity to a huge boulder. Though it sways on its pedestal, its jagged surfaces precariously balance one another, keeping their equilibrium. I suppose this means I'm an equilibrist walking a tightrope. My Catholic balancing act has made it easier to understand Buddhism, for none of it comes as a surprise: from Buddhist hells to the bliss of nirvana. Even Ash Wednesday's reminder of man as dust helps me grasp the Buddha's preaching of no underlying self. Zen Buddhists, if only they understood, would be enthralled at how Christian doctrine like a good koan stops thought in its tracks. In both traditions paradox is sanity."

"Is there any other doctrine keeping you a Catholic?"

"Yes, the communion of saints. Whenever I'm in Rome, I visit St. Peter's basilica. I like walking down the nave. I admire the towering statues on the lower and upper galleries reserved for the thirty-nine founders of religious orders. I always stop at two, St. Ignatius and St. Bruno. Ignatius holds the constitutions emblazoned with the initials, AMDG, *ad majorem Dei gloriam*—for the greater glory of God—while the trajectory of his right hand points to the Latin word, *legatum*, on the north wall of the nave. It comes from Matthew's Gospel in which Christ promises Peter that whatever he declares bound on earth will be bound [*legatum*] in heaven. Jesuits are to bind heaven to earth, the terrestrial to the celestial and the carnal with the spiritual. Ignatius enjoins his sons to worldly holiness. How different is Bruno the Carthusian off in a corner so suited to his solitude; he gazes at a skull while his foot crushes the bishop's miter he has firmly refused. Both men launched spiritualities paradoxically at odds with each other, yet both find a home in Catholicism. There are thirty-seven other founders from Teresa of Avila to Sophie Barat, for the church celebrates too the distaff side to holiness. Though all of them are fixed in stone, I feel their spirited presence as I amble up the nave."

"Do you have any final thoughts?"

"Yes. I take as my model Marguerite Yourcenar's encomium to Greek. I value comparative religion for the richness I find in the creed, cult, and code of Hinduism, Buddhism, Taoism, Confucianism, Judaism, and Islam. Each embodies the sacred in a coherent way of life. Everything humans have said or done best resides in the ethics and aesthetics of those six great religions. Nothing quite equals Islamic calligraphy, the Hebrew psalms, Taoist mystical paintings, Hindu temple sculptures, Zen Buddhist gardens, or Confucian social harmony. Together they enrich my life. But on my tombstone my epitaph, cut in Latin, will compress all that the spectator ever need know of me: that it was in the formative milieu of Catholicism I have thought and lived."

xii

Many of my novels and short stories involve one major human loss. A committed reader of my fiction pointed this out to me. "What accounts for the pattern of grief?" he asked. A facile answer would have been the death of my parents and several close friends, for I cannot disregard the impact on my life. But my brother's death stands out as the quintessential loss which affects my vision of things even when I'm writing comedy. I've dealt with my grief directly in the short story, "Gemini," which appears in *The Mansions of Limbo*. The narrative involves two identical twins who have recently lost their brothers and who meet through a *Times* obituary. The split screen of comparing similar accounts allowed me wide latitude in addressing my grief.

Like the twins in "Gemini," I was by age and experience closest to Michael, and stood by him at each stage of his illness. Despite the passage of two decades, the events of his death are still sharply etched, and something akin to resistance grips me whenever I summon them up. I offer these reflections out of fidelity to his memory. They may help my readers grasp the contours of Michael's life, especially his journey through the valley of chronic illness.

How does one isolate the mainspring of another's actions, how grasp its central motive? As a fiction writer, one gathers details, registers cause and effect, then constructs a plausible story. However astute the insight, no writer claims to penetrate fully a character's inner sanctum, but offers impressions that guide toward a convergent validity. With Michael, I can only offer a twin's version.

When I replay my memories of him, I ask myself if I sense some underlying issue or connecting link. Was it the dream of immortal youth, celebrity, and wealth? I don't deny what occupies many Americans. But I would add one further fundamental to his life: his relationship to Tolin. This young man was not just a partner in business; he was the center of my brother's world around which finance, family, and friends were satellites. In his shared life with Tolin, Michael sought to combine sensuality, tenderness, and friendship. But what should have been an occasion for growth became an impediment. If their relationship grew, it did so by shunting to the side everything else. It ousted much of the past—all those disciplined years in seminary—and set rigid boundaries for the present. Those who watched knew such exclusivity boded ill for the future. If Michael's life with Tolin oscillated between sweet-tempered and accusatory words, it was still one of unconditional allegiance. It brooked no rivals, not even a twin brother. And what was true for Michael was true for Tolin; the symbiosis came full circle. I use the psychological term advisedly, for their relationship had little to do with a bonding based on distinction of persons. Tolin and Michael overlapped. "We're in each other," my brother said with alarming candor. I was reminded of that terrifying scene in Bronte's *Wuthering Heights* when Cathy confesses to Ellen, "I am Heathcliff." The relationship was made to carry an impossible burden. The posture of clinging and dependency precipitated constant bickering, even occasional abuse—all aborted efforts to carve out separate identities. In the end, it took disease to divide them. Those who watched it coming with such velocity were powerless to stop it.

In reflecting on Michael's tragedy, which I read as a story of obsessive love, I find present what is prevalent in the population: a yearning for a perfect emotional alliance, some preeminent other who represents all that is or can be; who by definition is an image of beatific fulfillment. This absolutizing tendency—to cite William Lynch's apt expression—is at root the pursuit of the sacred in each of us. Today it has gone haywire in romanticism; in a word, idolatry. If Michael flouted any commandments of the Decalogue, the Sixth and Ninth are not what come to mind; it is the First: "I am the Lord, your God . . . no strange gods before you."

I have a photo of the two of them, side by side, with the ocean's surf breaking behind them. They are strikingly handsome, Michael and Tolin, and intelligent, funny, with boundless energy. Together they had launched a thriving business which they watched over like doting parents. Success had no boundaries. Like Gilgamesh and Enkidu of the Sumerian epic, they joined forces to vanquish the world. With wealth and health on their side, they seemed invincible. The height of glory was reached one night at Studio 54 when the fruits of their labor—images of the gorgeous and gifted—flashed across a colossal screen to the pleasure of guests who shared in the joint adulation. Shortly after this triumph, our heroes were brought very low. It took an onslaught of illnesses to tease them apart. Dying does that. It's something we do alone. If love reaches across the abyss, illness makes the other retreat to where no bridge can connect. Michael's dying fractured the relationship with Tolin, who was himself critically ill. They were in separate hospital beds on different floors. It was then that my brother turned to the inner guru and heard the still small voice whose volume through the years had become a murmur. The golden calf of human love was toppled and the covenant ark returned to its requisite niche. Michael reached for the one who outwaits (outwits?) all human lovers. The providential grace, of which G. K. Chesterton spoke in his admirable metaphor, had let Michael wander, but it pulled him back "with an unseen hook and a twitch upon the thread." How sad that in his midlife we could not pull him back or shake him to his senses. We coaxed and cajoled, counseled and cautioned. Nothing worked. His relationship with Tolin overrode everything. In the end, only God was empowered to tease them apart and get a hearing, the alone with the alone.

I miss my brother. For all his emotional investment in Tolin, he found time for acts of altruism and thoughtful concern. They came sometimes in spurts, sometimes in rivulets; but over a lifetime, they merged to become a torrent of affection. As I held him during his last hours, I recalled a poem written from seminary to celebrate our twenty-first birthday. Since then, I have reread it many times and give it here.

The Birthday

Under the sign of the Archer's tightened bow,
Like clashing figures in a violent dream
We challenged the world some twenty years ago,
Two variations on one martial theme.
Our strenuous cry, sent forth as nuncio,
Proclaimed to all our edict of esteem
For one who labored long to bring the earth
The customary miracle of birth.

Now, on the route of memory, I retrace
My footsteps round the spiraling years, until
I meet your mobile eyes and resolute face,
Like staunch St. Michael's on our windowsill.
Although you caught that statue's wiry grace,
With quick impassioned ways you managed still
To steal your mind against the commonplace,
To breathe an air unclaimed by natural breath
And shake both fists in the face of common death.

Sometimes I think, for all our restless ways,
And all those giddy heights we strove to climb,
Our eyes had glimpsed beyond declining days
How we might snatch eternity for time.
Yet some still wag their tongues in sullen praise,
Curling lips at the waste of manhood's prime,
As if we two could help being what we are:
Could we exchange the sun for a paler star?

I am no babbling prophet, yet aware
That though we disavowed one wedding feast,
Left name infertile with time, our only heir,
The stricken world takes us for spouse, at least,
To cleanse herself from cankerous despair;
As souring dough that take the cake of yeast
Grows fit for peddling in the market square.
There we with pauper, harlot, vagrant one
Shall journey, constant, under their tottering sun.

In the hour of his death, Michael made the journey and came home.

H aving spoken of my brother, I would like to speak of my sister, Joan. The homily I gave on the occasion of her silver anniversary, thirty years ago, sums up what I thought of her place in my life and family. I delivered it on October 22, 1978, during the Mass at which I presided.

Joan's Silver Anniversary: October 22, 1978

Everyone has a theory about her. She's too rigid, she's too free. She's a compulsive worker, she has too much fun. She's a loner, she's gregarious. She's the world's champion survivor, yet she manages somehow to emulate the Renaissance woman.

Her name comes up on campus because her religious certitude baffles her students. Hasn't she heard of the human condition? Yes, but she continues to challenge our categories. We prefer to think we're all in the same boat: slightly seasick, heading toward the turbulence; whereas she rarely loses track of the shoreline.

She's attractive, but she plays it down. In her view of things, to be too magnetic invites the world's attention. This is surely not her design.

She cultivates a no-nonsense style. Her clothes have that clean sort of line of a woman forever climbing in and out of a car to make herself useful at school or in church.

She moves with gusto. Her energy level is maintained, not by dance or exercise classes, but by the isometric tension of just keeping her spiritual balance.

When her face is in repose, she appears to be listening for something. I cannot make up my mind whether it is the sound of church bells or perhaps the rhythm of her pulse.

When she talks with us, her eyes meet ours with such generic enthusiasm, that she seems to look all around and through us as well as at us. And when she makes a point, her voice is steady: she intones her convictions.

Her conversation is confined to tangibles. She leans toward facts and is a touch impatient with speculation. When walking, she detours around sensuality, and this modesty lends freshness to all her gestures.

It is my impression that, after some twenty-five years of religious life, her womanliness centers on nurturing. I would guess that she is a much better pro at giving than receiving. For she has planted her students so deep in life, they cannot help but bloom. I suspect, too, that she supports her Jesuit colleagues more so emotionally, similar to a trellis that spreads like a fan. For me the most impressive thing about her is her closeness to music. It is the one place where her complete, sensuous self shows through. She looks at those piano keys as some women gaze at lovers; and when she translates notes into sound her face softens, and she moves as if she were the instrument being played.

Like so many academicians who have been schooled in the university, I'm always looking for structures; new paradigms to supplant those I feel intellectually bound to give up; however, she remains one of my constant images, a statue on the porch of a basilica. She helps me see the logic of religion like some figure in the corner of a medieval painting who points out the Christ to others. She is my lady theologian; in brief, my sister Joan.

Remarkable, isn't it, how the child is mother to the woman. Who could have guessed that the little five-year-old girl who refused to budge from a Kings Highway Street—who even then had a knack for stopping traffic—who could guess she would put such unbudgeability to such superb use? It is the stuff of which fidelity is made.

But enough of character analysis and whimsical flashbacks to childhood; the real motives underlying her life are largely scriptural. They are as trenchant as the Virgin's answer to Gabriel: "I am the Lord's servant. As you have spoken, so be it."

They are as pervasive as St. Paul's boast: "We are God's handiwork, created in Christ Jesus, to devote ourselves to good works."

They are as astute as the saying in the *Book of Wisdom* where we are told: "The sagacity of God is deemed more precious than the intelligence of men."

It is a dicey combination of motives: humility and service bound together by the knot of wisdom and developed human talents. Yet it makes for a vibrant attitude toward living. It produces a compassion that is never mindless, even when it inflexibly holds its ground. That is the woman, my sister, Joan. She is our antidote to complacency.

So when all systems fail: psychologies, sociologies, philosophies, and rituals; when to believe exclusively in one person, place, or thing is to be left like Adam—biting into the apple of discord with the taste of ashes on one's tongue—Joan's resiliency is everything. She has cultivated Mary's capacity for giving outright. She has learned from Christ how to die, if necessary, and to get up again. She knows, at heart, that everything is finally all right. She has told us over the years in so many deeds and words: "We follow not a system but a man. We pursue not an ideal but a vital spirit."

Dear Joanie:

On this, your twenty-fifth Silver Anniversary as a Sister of St. Joseph, we your family together with your friends and fellow religious, wish you our warmest congratulations and deepest affection our hearts can muster up. Even more, we extend to you our gratitude for the pride you give us in your many accomplishments; for the joy you exhibit artlessly in the face of living. As Dad would put it with a flick of his cigar: "That's *my* daughter—you know—the nun"; and while his possession remains intact, you have managed, nonetheless, to belong to us all.

Your loving brother,
Joseph

Photo Album

My grandfather and father, 1908

My paternal grandtparents' 50th wedding anniversary

My father, 1928, age twenty-two

My father at age twenty-six

Grandpa Martella, the carabiniere

My great grandparents, the Riccis, and Antoinette

Martella family, 1908; Lucie in front at two

1920 Graduation; Lucie 2nd row from top. 2nd from left

Mother, a sophomore at Julia Richmond H.S.

Lucie and Antointette, 1920

Lucie and Antoinette, 1927

Mother at eighteen, 1924

Lucie at 22 with Bette Davis eyes

Lucie and Anna's Cuban cruise, 1928

My parents' marriage, July 9, 1933

Uncle Paul, Best Man; Anna, Maid of Honor

My parents on their honeymoon

Cavalier Hotel, Virginia Beach, 1933

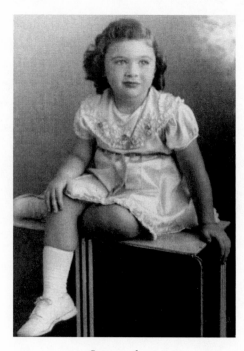

Joan at three

Aunt Emily at Joan's First Communion

Joan, 2nd row, 2nd from back

Aunt Mary holds Michael; Pina, me

Grandma Roccasalvo holds me;
my mother, Michael, at 4 months

Grandpa Roccasalvo with Michael and me at 8 months

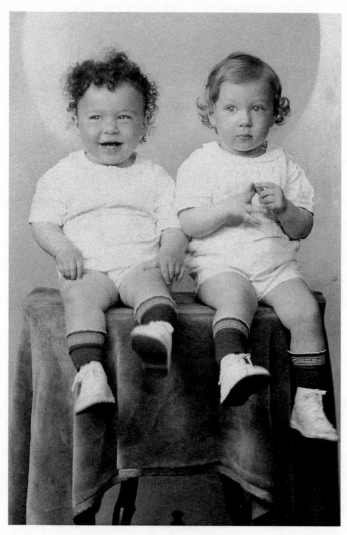

Joseph and Michael, 18 months

My family, 1943

My family, 1944

In front of our home, 1946

Grandma Martella, age 69, with Michael and me, 1947

First Communion with Father Joseph Lahey, 1949

Both grandfathers with my father, 1951

Graduation from St. Mark's, 1954

My parents on the Ocean Monarch to St. Lucia, 1964

Aunt Rita, 1933

Aunt Rita and mother, 1958

Joan in the habit of the Sisters of St. Joseph

Joan in suit and religious congregation's pin

James J. Hanley, S. J.
Latin, English, Book Store,
Freshman Sodality

Brooklyn Prep, 1954

Front Row: E. Szczepanski, J. Dearie, L. Bligh, P. Gambino, C. Mannix, J. McManus, R. Shea. *Second Row:* T. Fry, T. Fitzpatrick, W. Marwitz, W. Keller, W. Long, R. Romano, W. Hanlon. *Third Row:* L. Ockay, J. Colligan, W. Higgins, J. Guarrera, G. Shannon, J. Giordano, R. Kilichowski. *Fourth Row:* J. Roccosalvo, H. Connell, M. Roccosalvo, W. Burke, G. Owens, W. Reinecke, Mr. J. Hanley, S. J. *Back Row:* D. O'Connell, D. Chianchiano, V. Sclafani, J. Heggers, J. Sweeney, J. Sena, T. Crovello. *Not Pictured:* E. Cummings.

Freshman Class, 1955

Rev. Daniel J. Berrigan, S.J.
Religion, Latin, English
Senior Sodality

Brooklyn Prep, 1954

Daniel Berrigan, 1987, at 66

Vow Day with mother, 1960

My family, First Jesuit Vows, 1960

Vow Day with Michael, 1960

The three of us, Christmas, 1966

Laying on of hands by Cardinal Cooke, June 14, 1975

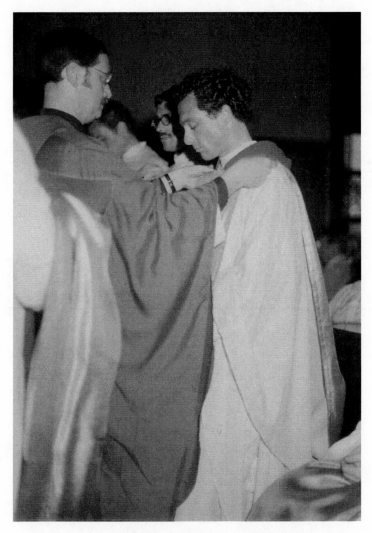

Receiving the priest's stole

First Mass, June 22, 1975, at St, Mark's Church

Dinner reception after First Mass

Michael's portrait of me, 1976

Graduation with Harvard Ph.D., June 8, 1978

Rome, 1982

With Joanna Datillo, celebrating my Ph.D., 1978

With Joanna celebrating birthdays, 2003

Maureen McCafferty

Maureen McCafferty

Lucie with friend, Jacob, at the St. Regis, Christmas, 1998

Tolin Green, 1978

Michael, 1978

Michael, 1982

Michael and Tolin, 1982

With Joan at the Baur au Lac, Zurich, 1998

Lugano, Switzerland, 1998

With Dan Conlin, Rome, 2000, 25 years a priest

Part II

Passato Prossimo

i

In 1984, I flew from Paris to Grenoble and took a local bus to the small village of St. Pierre de Chartreuse in the Dauphiné Alps. I was researching "a spiritual thriller" based on the elixir of long life, the reputed base of the green and yellow liqueurs called *chartreuse*; it later became the one word title of the novel. I offer the reader a summary from the book's flap:

> Historically founded on a sixteenth century alchemist's elixir of long life (and the basis for the French liqueur), CHARTREUSE is a story of supernatural transformation; of the elixir's ingredients on which a Pope's life rests; of a young man's destiny and the chain of world events that lead to his final, wrenching choice.
>
> The central character, Blaise, is summoned to Switzerland once he learns he has inherited a parchment containing the recipe for nothing less than the elixir of life. He's directed to a distiller in the French countryside—a Carthusian monk at La Grande Chartreuse—for he alone knows how "to execute the formula to the greater glory of God and humanity."

At the same time, someone wants the Pope dead and has infected him with a fatal disease. So the race is on: to save the Pope; to see which woman will accompany Blaise during his travails—his current lover, or a flame from his past; to discover if the culprit can keep the elixir from reaching the Vatican.

CHARTREUSE is fast paced without being frantic. And yet, in the drawing power of the plot's twists and turns, so much more than a plot goes on: a romance, a thriller, a source book of homeopathy, miraculous events, a spiritual journey. It's a search for a cure; a search for a moral code; a search for identity. With CHARTREUSE, Joseph Roccasalvo has written a novel about the sacred and profane—a contemporary symbol of our 21st century lives.

Each afternoon, I left the Beau Site hotel where I was staying and trekked to the seat of the Carthusian order at La Grande Chartreuse three miles away. In depicting the monastic composition of place, my efforts were nothing new. For years, I had conducted my morning meditation in the same manner, imagining Jesus and his disciples in sensuous contact with their Judean environment. Once again—this time for literary reasons—I enlisted the five senses together with mind and heart. I was intent on writing fiction for the whole person. I never forgot what Bob Giroux of Farrar Strauss & Giroux had told my literary agent. After reading *Fire in a Windless Place*, he remarked: "Roccasalvo has Somerset Maugham's talent for paying close attention to the setting. He is generous with details. He makes you feel you're there." As a seminarian, I had learned the knack of immersion by taking St. Ignatius at his word: to be so steeped in the living scene that I became a bystander to Christ's fasting in the desert, his call of the Twelve, the cure of the centurion's son, or the release of the adulteress from stoning. Jesuit contemplation was a form of "you are there."

That morning in the Dauphiné Alps, as I walked up the monastic road in the Zone of Silence, I memorized the environment. I listened to the cowbells, inhaled the scented air, and felt the soft breeze buffet my face. When I reached the monastery's front door and rang for the porter, he opened it and allowed me passage into the courtyard. The Carthusian master of novices met me, and together we walked to a guest parlor where we conversed. After sharing my biography with him, I mentioned my adolescent desire to join his order.

"In your case, Joseph, it would have been a serious mistake. You did well to ignore it. You would never have stayed." His reply sounded like a reproach.

"I'm not sure I understand. Is it because of my academic background? Your own founder, St. Bruno, was a renowned teacher and one of Cologne's academic lights. He was involved with the world."

"True, but he later found his calling in what is the hallmark of our order: solitude. It opens us completely to God if we're receptive. In prayer, we dispense with images in a cloud of unknowing whereas your active imagination multiplies them. Our vocation involves long stretches of silence while yours enjoins communicating with words."

I've returned often to that alpine conversation about my errand in the world. Once again a religious superior had admonished me with the truth.

ii

W henever I do a reading from one of my books for a class of students or for members of a book club, I dramatize the words of the characters in such a way that it seems I know them. While performing the text adds the ring of realism, it also invites curiosity. Invariably I'm asked if I knew them. It's not unlikely that they've come to the session of Meet the Author with a scene from a novel in mind. Perhaps it's Guigo bent on killing a pope by lethal injection; or maybe it's Guido threatening a woman with a pistol in a Swiss graveyard. It could also be the beach encounter between Mark and Benedict that heightens their interest. "Are you really reporting events in which you shared?" The word "really" is their way of asking, "Did this happen to you?"

"Yes, it did," I reply, "but in my imagination."

The answer proves unsatisfactory because it sounds evasive as if I'm refusing to be candid about my sources. To them that can mean only one thing, my lived experience. Some readers have to grasp that an imagined experience is truly an experience. But because I have invested the papal murder, the scene in the cemetery, or the acrobatics of sex with such intensity, it's concluded I'm recounting events in which I have participated. Sometimes I forestall the error with words about the craft of writing; how many events are collapsed into one, or how the qualities of many people combine to form a unitary character.

"It's a composite portrait drawn from many models," I say in summary. It still sounds evasive.

"But where does your story come from? Scenes follow one another as if they were always there."

"If you're asking me whether there's any basis in fact, yes, there is. Usually it's from something that's deeply affected me. Afterward I ask myself: What does this mean? What am I being told? Let me offer you one incident that's still an enigma. It will sound farfetched but it truly happened."

"At the twentieth anniversary of my brother's death, during the second week of October, I went to Union Square Park to sit and read. I wanted to distract myself from the loss weighing me down. I was unable to shake off the gloom. I took with me a signed edition of Iris Murdoch's *The Bell*. The book was in mint condition with its original dust jacket in shrink wrap. I found a bench and sat down next to Harry, a friend from the gym. Having greeted me, he left me to read while he conversed with a Greek man, a park devotee. While they were chatting, I looked at the novel's dust jacket. It seemed rather odd considering the title of the book. Instead of the novel's monastic bell adorning the cover, a young girl was pictured with her hands releasing a butterfly into the air. Her face was ecstatic as she watched the emancipated butterfly take flight."

"While studying the image, a monarch butterfly fluttered overhead and landed on the book cover near the butterfly's drawing. It remained there for several seconds, then, with its wings splayed, proceeded to crawl up my hand and arm to my shoulder. For several seconds it remained there while its wings rhythmically opened and closed. Sitting next to me, Harry looked over and reacted by nudging his Greek companion in my direction. The scene became more singular as the butterfly came and went five times before it vanished from sight. The occurrence nonplussed the three of us. I noted the time of the incidence. It was seven fifteen. The butterfly ritual had taken five minutes before it ended."

"I do not know what possessed me but at seven the next evening I walked over to Union Square Park. I was in luck. The bench of the night before was vacant. I sat down and waited. Presently, at seven ten the monarch butterfly reappeared. It came and went, fluttering overhead, and only once alighting on my hand remained motionless. It then flew away as mysteriously as it appeared.

"Was it the same airborne creature that had visited me the day before? I'm not a lepidopterist, and my entomological interests are nil. To my untutored vision, there was nothing to distinguish it as unique. It may well have been the same butterfly. Utterly astonished, I tried to understand what happened and why. I hastened home and phoned a friend who is gifted at interpreting uncanny events."

"What were you feeling when you arrived at the park yesterday?"

"A sense of loss; I was missing my brother."

"And after the butterfly came and went, how did you feel?"

"Peaceful."

"Perhaps you were being told through the butterfly that Michael is all right. As the caterpillar leaves the cocoon and goes from an earthly to a heavenly creature, so Michael now has a new life while remaining present to you. It's still his manner to flit in and out but this time he's letting you know all is well."

A week later, I was at Barnes & Noble bookstore. At the magazine rack, I picked up the latest issue of *The Economist*. I was scanning the section that listed new releases when I saw a review of a book on butterflies. The opening paragraph grabbed my attention. According to the reviewer, the archaic Greek word for butterfly was *psuche*, which later became the Greek word for soul or vital spirit. Had Michael used the butterfly to scatter my gloom and communicate his peace? Was he saying that his living spirit was with me?

By sharing an actual occurrence, I'm offering the reader the premise of a still unwritten story. Henry James's "what if" sets the events in motion. My imagination may nudge the story along with contrasting viewpoints—spiritualism, agnosticism, and mysticism—until I arrive at the literary truth I have intended.

Another cause that provokes a story may be an inquiry whose broad concern is no less than everything. What comes to mind is a question posed by the secretary of my former literary agent. In the process of sending out manuscripts, he decided to read everything I had written. More than halfway through the corpus, he said to me, "You know, Joseph, I can feel a pattern in your stories. They no longer surprise me. I don't mean I'm not jolted by the twists and turns. You still make me turn the page. What I'm saying is that I can tell it's you by the content."

"What do you think I'm saying?" I asked.

"You mean, is there an underlying story?"

"You could put it that way."

"I'd have to bring your characters together and ask them. They'd know since they've lived through the events."

"Maybe I should invite them for a weekend away. I'm sure they would oblige and answer your question."

"Which one is that?"

"What did I have in mind when I imagined them?"

On the basis of this conversation, I outlined a novella I called *A Weekend Away* in which all fifty characters from my novels and short stories are provided airline tickets and asked to come to the Villa Roccasalvo on Lake Como for a holiday extending from Friday evening until Monday morning. After cocktails and a buffet dinner, where the characters are free to sit at random and hobnob, Roccasalvo descends the staircase during post-prandials and addresses them:

"It warms my heart to see you together in the same place," he begins, and so invites the applause of his cast of characters.

"You may be wondering what accounts for this get together. It's taken some imagination to find a story in which you comfortably fit. Now that I'm living the last part of my life, I needed an excuse to bring you all here."

"All?" someone asks. "Aren't you likely to create more characters? You've just begun a new work called *The Sign of the Archer* in which a man with a talent for deciphering languages wakes up one morning to find he can decipher people. You've named him Justin Sinclair and gifted him with the third eye. Won't he miss out on being here?"

"Technically you're right. But I prefer working with characters already fleshed out. You fifty will do. You're a large enough group from whom I may ask a communal favor. First-class plane tickets, superior lodging, and superb cuisine do not come without demands. I think you'll find my request beguiling. Let me explain.

"In this weekend away—from tonight until Monday morning—I would like you to break up into five groups of ten people. They should be of mixed gender to allow for a diverse response. Choose someone from each group to record what's said and then submit the remarks to a panel of five. They will summarize the comments in order to answer one question: What did I intend when I created you? And in the creation, was I candid and revealing, or opaque and concealing? Furthermore, if you can embody your answer in a visual symbol, I would be thrilled.

"I'll leave you now to begin your review. Be surgical where you must, but probe compassionately. It's not a cadaver, but a vital person you're exploring who wishes his life enhanced by what you learn. The Sanskrit proverb will be your guide: 'The truth will out.'"

Another basis for literary invention is the friendship that develops as a result of mentoring. Since I no longer teach full-time, I look for pedagogical outlets and go to places where students are likely to assemble like college dining halls and cafés. I enter and stand in line to buy my coffee as I search the tables, especially those in corners commandeered by readers. If they have loaded the table with cell phone, iPod, computer or BlackBerry, and disinvited the outside by using ear phones, *per forza*, I turn my attention elsewhere. However engaging the impending conversation, it cannot compete with gadgets each geared to the semblance of intimacy. It is rare to find readers alone with a book and nothing else. I make concessions for one technological tool but nothing more, and I note how often it's used. If the book dominates the reader by its content, I position myself alongside and casually ask when the person looks up:

"Is it a classic?" and then await the answer. It's a safe bet that a Penguin edition meets the case. Sometimes I ask a more telling question:

"Are you?"

"Am I what?"

"A classic. It takes one to know one."

The remark should elicit a smile. If the facial reaction is quizzical, I have erred in my initial judgment. But the book is living evidence. If someone is reading Oscar Wilde's *The Picture of Dorian Gray* or Cicero's *Orations* in Latin—and this may demand a café in Harvard Square—I have landed a literary light. Any text in the original language is a hook for conversation. It may proceed with a question from my anonymous reader:

"It all depends on what you mean by 'classic.'"

"Excellent," I reply. "But I warn you. Break the circle at any point and you're involved with nothing less than everything. Are you game?"

"Yes."

The book closes. Even the cell phone is removed from sight, a clear sign that I will not have divided attention. The conversation shifts from the book's story to ours.

"I'll take a stab at the word 'classic' and see if we overlap in definition. It's something that serves as a standard of recognized value. It's enduring like classic architecture or even classic tailoring. The word was first used in Greek or Roman culture to mean the highest class. I use it to refer to something of sustained excellence like *The Odyssey*, *The Iliad*, or *The Aeneid*, classics of the first rank."

If the conversation continues and we agree to meet again over an academic concern—choosing a career or graduate school—a foundation for mentoring has been established. Much later, sometimes years, what began as a form of counseling emerges as a story. In Appendix I of this memoir, I offer *The Fourth Letter*. It's a fictionalized version of a real café encounter in which the mentoring became a preamble to a friendship long after the academic goal was realized. The story's Marcus Hoffmann is a disguised version of me; the eulogy offered at the story's end is an occasion for poking biographical fun.

A still further resource for a story may be lines drawn from a classic novel, for example, *Helena* by Evelyn Waugh. In the chapter called "Epiphany," Helena, the mother of Constantine the Great, ruminates over the three wise men from the east who journeyed to Bethlehem to see the infant savior. The discoverer in her eighties of the True Cross, the empress Helena sees herself like them, a procrastinator, who has found her calling in her dotage. She calls the wise men "the patron saints of all latecomers." I asked myself what preceded their meandering journey; what made them late in arriving. So I wrote *An Open Letter to the Magi* on a theme from Evelyn Waugh and offered an imaginative answer; I presumptuously altered Waugh's faultless prose to realize my intent. I've used the letter successfully each year on the Epiphany. As a comparative religionist and historian of religions, I view that Sunday as my titular feast. I offer the letter as evidence of my manner in "sermonizing."

Dear Gaspar, Melchior, and Balthasar:

Today, late in the morning, a group of friends and I gathered to hear the recent installment of your celebrated pilgrimage westward. Our mutual friend, Matthew the Jew, who is gifted in the art of reportage, provided us with the necessary details, how one week after the birth of the carpenter's son, you managed to complete the hazardous journey you began so many months ago. Naturally, we were overjoyed you had arrived without harm to mind or person. As we listened to Matthew's account, we felt intense esteem, especially for your courage in having attempted the trip at all, for the weather has been nasty, the countryside bleak, and the swamps, jungles, and mountain ranges have all conspired to make your hope capricious.

I, for one, who am acquainted with your good taste in living and dining, can appreciate the irksomeness of your journey. I know too well how rarely you travel beyond the confines of your kingdoms. It is then with some astonishment that I imagine you three processing over highland and valley in your costly brocades, with your venerable faces like rutted stone, and all that paraphernalia clanging side by side. It is with amusement, too, that I picture you in the evenings, reclining under a makeshift canopy, yearning for your slippers and missing terribly your wives, books, and late hour aperitif. How pervasive habits can be, and how admirable under adversity not to renege on commitment.

But I must be candid with you. I admit that I've never been clear about the reasons why you three undertook this journey with such a demonstration of resolve. I could assign causes: your obsession with astrology, your toying with the occult, and your general proclivity for bright stars. But listening to your version, I alter my opinion. I believe you when you say the journey had to do with dissatisfaction, as if a domesticated animal were scratching at the back of the mind restless to get out of doors. It may have to do with living in those drafty palaces and hearing as you dozed the drip of the faucet, the creak of the mattress, and the wind in the attic repeating the same question: What does it all mean?

Those of us this morning who have made the same pilgrimage—admittedly at shorter distances and at much less cost than your own—have an overall sense why you three journeyed to Bethlehem. The geography of your world, however exotic, is not so different from our own. Whatever our lineage, all of us share the same human condition and cope with the same mortality. Though we are neither the descendants of kings nor feel the weight of royal prerogatives, we, too, have labored at tasks we do not relish, lived with people we find disagreeable, and indulged our appetites to satisfy an unappeasable hunger. Most of us have received too little affection in our lives or given too much. It seems our collective destiny to become masters in the arts of unrequited love.

What you share with us more immediately is that you were late in arriving at Bethlehem. The shepherds and their flocks had come days before. They had added their voices to the angelic chorale before you arrived on the scene. To hasten your coming, the sovereignty of the stars was diminished, and a more imperious light commanded the heavens.

How judiciously you came, checking maps and measurements, where the shepherds had rushed headlong. How bizarre you appeared on the road prodding on your pack animals weighed down with such incongruous gifts. You finally came to the last stage of your journey, pausing to visit King Herod, and in that icy interchange of courtesies, there began the cold war of attrition against the powerless.

Nonetheless, you arrived and were not sent away. Your gifts were unnecessary but graciously received, for they were given outright. In that democracy of love so recently established, there was room for royalty too.

You were not less equal in the eyes of the Holy Family than the sheep or the goat.

Gaspar, Melchior, Balthasar, you are our elected saints, the patrons of all latecomers: of all who journey fitfully toward the truth; of all who get entangled in the thickets of reflection; of all who through caution become accessories to evil; of all who are imperiled by virtue of their talents.

Dear cousins, pray for us, that we before the end may find room on the manger floor. For the sake of the Child who did not refuse your improbable gifts, intercede for us: the constant, the indifferent, the wavering, that we may not be quite forsaken at the gates of Heaven when the just inherit the Kingdom.

iii

A friend of mine who recently visited my Web site remarked on the number of books I've written over two decades. He phoned me saying he wanted to talk about it. We agreed to meet for coffee at an outdoor café. He's a superb writer, but says he's begun to feel his age. This means he has good days and bad days, and of late the bad ones prevail. As we sipped our cappuccinos in a quiet corner, he described how he sits before a blank page in what he calls a literary stupor.

"With my mind in a dead halt, the words don't come. Like an insomniac leaving a disheveled bed, I rise from my chair and pace and then try sitting again to write. But I force myself, so nothing happens. I'm unable to bump start my imagination. And when I turn to other writers for inspiration and read a passage; for example, Maugham's description of the elegant Isabel in *The Razor's Edge*, or Waugh's of the wistful Julia in *Brideshead Revisited*, the fluency of the language incapacitates me further. What's worse, Joseph, than a writer who can't write; who feels the day stretching before him in a formless void. So when I view your Web site, I find your output enviable. You've been prolific. But you're careful about your health. You go for regular checkups: your annual physical, your eye exam, and your quarterly visit with the dentist. You have it down to a ritual. I don't get the sense you obsess about being well. You take being healthy for granted."

"You may be granting me more than I do myself. I have to be well. I'm responsible to too many people."

"I don't understand. You're not married. You're currently not teaching, and you have no dependents."

"You're missing a major group. The characters in my book depend on me. If I'm dyspeptic, so are they. If I'm emotionally focused, they are too. They speak and act in character and don't go off on a tangent, testing the reader's credibility. Because I trust my imagination, the reader can trust me. It's axiomatic. It comes from living with calculable regularity."

"You've used that expression often."

"It's a summary phrase."

"What does it sum up?"

"A life in balance without addictions."

"Fiction writers are reputed to cultivate at least one. I think of Hemingway and Fitzgerald, not to mention a playwright like Tennessee Williams. Literature gives them the right to drink and smoke, fornicate and overeat."

"Sorry to disappoint. To cite a Buddhist adage, I like to pull in my fires and not consume what's around me like a California blaze. It helps that I have a fixed routine. Whenever it's fractured, I'm at odds with myself. I need to exercise in a gym at the start and end of the day, especially if I've been writing for hours. It keeps me from feeling edgy."

"How does your schedule run?"

"Since I need eight hours of sleep, I'm in bed before midnight and up by eight. If it's a nice day a cup of coffee accompanies me to the park along with my polyglot version of Luke's Gospel. I received it as a gift from the Palazzo Sasso in Ravello, a thousand feet above the Amalfi Coast. The book is suited to someone like me who enjoys maneuvering among several tongues. I like to hear Jesus speak Italian at Cana, consort with sultry women in Spanish, preach the Sermon on the Mount in French, and be tried by Pilate in German."

"And English?"

"If a word's meaning escapes me, I check the English for precision. Occasionally I bring my *Novum Testamentum Graece et Latine* and read the text in Greek and Latin. It keeps me in touch with the sources."

"Does all this linguistic movement qualify as prayer?"

"It leads to a combined insight focusing my day. If spiritual writers, East and West, agree that prayer is engagement with the sacred, it's heightened by several languages together."

"And as a novelist concerned with moral and religious themes, does it benefit you?"

"Yes. When I move from one version to the next, I have the sense that the Gospel story belongs to the world. Its significance is global. The genius of world religions is that their narratives are 'concrete universals.' As languages of the spirit, they belong to us globally even when their origins stem from a unique time and place. So if Buddha gained enlightenment for Buddhists, he did so finally for all men and women; if Jesus gained salvation for Christians, he did so ultimately for all men and women. My childhood prepped me for shuttle diplomacy among religions while Harvard honed the ability. Like the man who acts as interpreter between foreign heads of state, I view myself as a religious go-between—the person in the middle making dialogue possible. I'm never more central than when I disappear."

iv

"How do you find this balance? Maybe that's my question with writer's block. Something in me is out of joint and wants integration."

"Balance is external and results from what's internal, namely, harmony. The great religions offer ways to talk about this transcendent state. Taoists stress the mutual enrichment of yang with yin while Buddhists affirm the complementary powers of wisdom with compassion; the Confucian sage insists on social harmony derived from the five relationships. Human beings have been historically inventive when trying to describe what creates perfect concord. Even in Christianity, the Church Fathers differentiated between *anima, animus,* and *spiritus*: the animal, rational, and spiritual, depending on which function dominated the individual. In my novel, *Fire in a Windless Place,* Alexander Corbett refers to them as 'the three steeds of the self' which he steers 'toward some impossible perfection.' Alex too was striving for an integrated life."

"Is harmony a question of inner refinement?"

"No. It results in something of such consummate excellence that it seems to be literally out of this world. The characteristics are always the same. They are best described by a first experience I had auctioning trophy wines from the Bordeaux and Burgundy regions of France. They included all the 1998 *premiers grands crus classés* and *grands vins* of the

Vosne-Romaneé. After paying the commission on their sale, I walked away with a profit four times my original investment. I was astonished at the rise in value within a decade of their purchase. I paged through the catalogue in which the wines were featured to learn why they commanded such inflated prices. Much later, when I sold two rare books and a photograph and letter of a British author, I isolated the attributes of what makes something great. They were always together."

What more I said by way of explanation I will share with the reader. Whether dealing with estate wines, rare books, or famous autographs, the same characteristics pertain. They hold true for stamps and also for coins of which I have a limited knowledge. In each case I was dealing with something of such recognized value it was considered the best of the best. The unrivaled *quality* was known as such. Of limited quantity, the auctionable wines possessed *rarity*. This proved obvious when only six thousand bottles were produced and oenologists had rated the vintage A or A+. The wines' reputation was often legendary with a history of distinction. I could count on *desirability* by those with enough savoir-faire to acknowledge their status. The passage of time, resulting in diminished numbers, enhanced the *marketability* by increasing their value.

I'm advancing nothing original when I say these characteristics apply to the great arts: from painting and sculpture to architecture and literature. I would add to the list great lives. I turn to wine as my primary analogy because it features so prominently in the Gospel and is a key element in Christian liturgy. When properly paired with food in a lovely environment, it is an enhancement to friendship.

A great wine's perfect balance and aromatic complexity remind me of the outstanding life that seems to happen as a kind of grace. That power of richness, purity, and intricate refinement which makes a wine "long in the mouth" also makes a human life, memorably lived, "long in the memory." The aura of greatness surrounding a wine derives not only from age and experience, but also from the *terroir's* unique mix of soil, slope, and incline of sun. I do not think it farfetched to view a great human life as a fine vintage. Inspired living has its own rigors resembling those of winemakers who punish the vine—*punir la vigne* in the admirable French phrase—cutting back ruthlessly on the stem to limit the growth. It may result in a paucity of grapes, but it guarantees intensity, concentration, and longevity.

Quality, rarity, and desirability characterize the places of residence where I go for a holiday. I mean the great hotels whose brochures are an invitation to share another kind of harmony. I reminisce about them often: Il Pellicano, the Palazzo Sasso, the Hotel Splendide, the Baur au Lac, the Grand Hotel Tremezzo, the Grand Hotel Villa Igeia, the Villa Castagnola, the Hotel Splendido, the Hotel de Russie, and the Kempinski Giardino di Costanza; all of them share the attribute of being unforgettable. Opulence is not what fixes them in memory—they are far from the flamboyance of Las Vegas—but a balance of sense and spirit in which each complements the other.

Brochures picture these hotels in landscapes graced by shrubs in tiered gardens and blessed with views of the sea and mountains. An outdoor pool enjoys the panorama. Each hotel is a small paradise inducing contemplative calm. There is nothing hurried here, no daily schedule to pressure you; just an attentive staff that makes you feel at home. For these are livable spaces like elegantly appointed homes where comforts, taken for granted, become a state of mind. The antiques, paintings, and sculpture at the San Domenico Palazzo in Taormina entice the guest indoors. I have walked down the carpeted hallways as though in a museum's gallery, observing how the art is tastefully paired with the interiors.

The hotels are usually close to a metropolitan area. After a buffet breakfast and a morning stroll under trees dappled by sunlight, I collapse in a deck chair to recover. Soon I will sacrifice the perfect geometry of the pool to visit the urban center a few miles away. City and country cooperate to offer the best of both worlds. After a day of sightseeing, I return to the hotel to enjoy dinner's inventive cuisine. Served on the terrace, the main course is preceded by sampling a peppery or herbaceous olive oil; or tasting an exquisite hors d'oeuvre sent by the chef to tease the palate. The two hour dinner that follows is prolonged by the regional wine, and ends with a plate of sweets notable for their symmetric arrangement.

A week in one of these prelapsarian Edens is all that's needed to integrate mind and body, and to prove Oscar Wilde right that the soul is cured by the senses and the senses by the soul. When I finally return home to New York, I take refuge from the frenetic pace by conjuring up my vacation. Memory ensures its real presence like the small red flame in the copper lamp on a Catholic altar.

"It sounds awfully expensive, Joseph," my writer friend interjects. "Yours is a holiday few can afford."

"I admit perfection doesn't come cheaply. But instead of staying in charmless hotels for three weeks, shorten your stay to one. Better to drink fine wine for one week than jug wine for three."

"It's still costly. How do you justify it?"

"Travel is part of the writer's vocation. In these hotels I meet engaging people who prime my stories. But something else motivates me. On my deathbed, will I repent having stayed in Portofino or Porto Ercole? Or lament having gazed at the Ionian or Mediterranean seas from the cliffs of Taormina or Ravello? I don't think so. Invest in your memories. Together with deeds motivated by kindness, they are all you have to speed you on your way. Furthermore, you'll more happily move into one of the mansions promised by the Gospel if you've first stayed at a fine hotel; it eases the passage from one paradise to the next."

V

I travel by myself. Occasionally, I meet friends in Rome or Milan for a predinner drink and the rendezvous is always pleasurable. But I resemble Somerset Maugham who was a solitary traveler. When I examine his stories, I find him invariably alone, but porous to making acquaintances. My single presence appears singular to people who travel in twos. I have a knack for attracting couples who are drawn to my background, and who invite me to join them.

The first husband and wife who schooled me in involvement with happily married couples were my uncle Artie and aunt Rita. My memory of them dates back to those evenings when they phoned my parents to say they would stop by for Mother's superb spaghetti dinner. They enjoyed eating late at our kitchen table, just the two of them, and holding court with my parents who had dined earlier. Before they said good-bye, my brother and I would be summoned to share a twenty-dollar bill that Rita ceremoniously tore in half, giving one side of President Jackson to each of us. Surgical reconstruction of the president came later.

They married early when Rita was eighteen and Artie a few years older. Perhaps he first saw her at the 21 Club where she worked as a hatcheck girl; or perhaps he met her at a cabaret where she demonstrated modern dance. From the start, theirs was a devoted but stormy relationship. They divorced at least once, separated several times, but like swans that mated for life they returned to each other. Artie doted on Rita even when they shared one room at the Keteri Nursing Home run by the archdiocese. It was a grim environment in which they ate tasteless, tepid meals, and a far cry from the dining they had enjoyed near Lincoln Center where they lived in a rent-controlled apartment. The maintenance was so low it made the building's owner apoplectic with rage. He could have received thousands for their three-room flat for which they paid two hundred dollars a month. During their middle years, I saw them often as nephew; as they aged, sporadically as an adult. I was with them in the emergency room at the end. I said their funeral Masses, preached their eulogies, and consigned their remains to the ground where they are buried side by side. What I remember most was how much Artie loved Rita, and how she took that love for granted. He was there for her through sixty marital years whose turbulence was more a sign of vitality than disaffection.

My uncle dressed smartly in the way men did in the forties, aping the sartorial perfection of Fred Astaire or Cary Grant: white shirt, silk tie, double-breasted suit with pocket square, and shoes buffed to a high sheen. He was a retired policeman who had suffered a bullet to his skull while pursuing a criminal, and he had survived the skirmish. He displayed the cranial cavity like a badge of honor. Although he belonged to the New York police force, he resembled in profile the cinematic gangster George Raft; they might have been taken for twins. Though he was dashing in person, he viewed himself as a gilt-edged frame to exhibit his wife. If Artie resembled a Hollywood star, Rita was the celebrity.

She was baptized Rafaela. In school they nicknamed her Rae. Her teachers addressed her by what they assumed was her real name, Rachel. For half my life I knew her as Aunt Rachel. But when she began dancing professionally in nightclubs, my mother gave her the stage name, Rita Clavell; so for the second half of my life she was Aunt Rita. Of all the Martella girls—and each was striking in appearance—Rita was the most alluring. Her jet black hair had a white streak that she said appeared overnight after being stalked in Central Park. She swept the hair back from her face with tortoise shell combs studded with rhinestones. Her flawless skin, green eyes, and lashes darkened by mascara were features that sufficed to turn one's head. But the dimpled smile and pearly white teeth were her hallmark. As vivacious as she was entrancing, it was impossible not to notice her. She lit up the room.

Rita preferred wearing black sheath dresses from Saks Fifth and sling back heels from I. Magnin. She kicked them off during a solo routine as she shimmied and shook in her stocking feet. Slender but curvaceous, and lithe as a cat, she was riveting on the ballroom floor where her improvised movements made a dance partner redundant.

"She's the most glamorous of the Martella girls," spectators said, and in the saying provoked competitive outbursts from Rosie, Yetta, and Louise who each laid claim to the title.

Rita had a wicked tongue. Despite her decorous manner, in later life she often became unhinged and resorted to expletives that could make a seasoned cop blush. She was always at odds with someone in the family, especially my grandmother's sister, Antoinette, who from her earliest years had played my mother's advocate. Rita ridiculed Antoinette by focusing on the scoliosis of the spine that had severely hunched her. The insults persisted to such a degree that Mother refused to speak with her.

"Rita's nothing but a troublemaker," was her summary judgment, and the two remained incommunicado. She was the only sister not invited to my priestly ordination.

Rita was especially fond of my father. Though she was not on speaking terms with my mother when he died in 1976, she appeared at the funeral home, unexpected and unannounced. In the parlor where he was waked, she made her grand entrance in black mink while Artie followed behind. Approaching my mother, Rita forestalled any objection by declaring:

"Lucie, I loved your husband. Mike was a *good* man. I came to pay my respects."

It was a tense moment. At the time Rita was on the outs, not only with Mother, but also with Louise, Rosie, and Yetta who were present at the wake. Rita knelt and said a prayer before the open casket. She rose to face a hostile family, words were exchanged, and the wrangling that followed continued into the street. Appalled by the scene, Mother repeated her earlier judgment: "She's nothing but trouble. She brings it wherever she goes."

Prior to this incident and before I left for seminary, I was Rita's favorite nephew. "I love this kid," she used to say, and then pulled me close in a tight embrace. I inhaled her perfume and felt her body in its costly dress; a dress, by the way, which arrived in Mother's closet. Rita tired of her expensive clothes and gave them to Mother who shared her size. Designer suits, silk dresses, even furs which my mother could never have afforded hung in her closet.

Rita joined me at Grand Central Station before my parents and I took the nine-hour trip to Plattsburgh where I entered the seminary. I remember the tearful good-bye. It pleased her that I planned to be a priest. Could she have foreseen that I would be at her deathbed to absolve and anoint her? Decades later I was summoned to the emergency room where I stood alongside as she gasped for air. Looking gaunt and haggard, she was the great beauty now crushed by adversity. The words of Auden echoed in my mind: "Time is indifferent in a week to a beautiful physique." What a lesson in impermanence. And yet the faded person lying there as the summation of her prior selves could not dim the memory that trumped them all: of the exorbitant woman who was both spouse and free spirit, exhibition dancer and my ardent admirer. Of all my aunts, she schooled me in the joy of being singled out and chosen for love. Her glamour decided my preference for women who move in an aura of scent. When they finally depart, the fragrance fosters an easy remembrance.

My aunt and uncle exemplified what ensures longevity in marriage: one that reinvents itself for better or worse and commits a couple to a continuously shared history. Auden's abstract definition of love proves true: "intensity of attention joined to complicity of emotion." Husband and wife may be in love, but they must genuinely *like* each other. Sexual attraction springs from their mutual enjoyment and celebrates it.

Besides my uncle and aunt, another couple comes readily to mind. My regency as a Jesuit teacher began in 1965 at Brooklyn Prep and lasted for three years. During that time I became close friends with Gabe and Grace Cucolo. He was head of the Lutheran Medical Center and a first-rate doctor. His wife Grace who helped arrange their social life kept him well with surprise vacations that eased his grueling schedule. They played golf on courses around the world.

I met her at prep on parents' night after the students had returned from Christmas vacation. She came over and waited in line to speak with me. She had heard me mentioned favorably by parents whose sons I instructed. Though I did not have her son in class, she wanted me to take an interest in Richard whose attitude bewildered her. She knew I would accompany him to France the following summer. I was slated to chaperone prep's students while Father John Ferrand, head of the language department, settled details about dorm living, classes in French and Parisian sightseeing. When her turn finally came, Grace walked over and sat down.

"You're, Mr. Roccasalvo?"

"Yes."

"You're a Jesuit scholastic?"

"Yes."

"I'm Grace Cucolo, the mother of that bloke you see over there. Do you think you can do something with him? I'm out of ideas."

"I don't have your son in class, but I'll be with him this summer, Mrs. Cucolo."

"That's six months from now. By the way, call me Grace. May I call you Rock?"

"Yes, but don't let anyone hear you."

"You know, Rock, Richard could use some guidance. My husband and I can't seem to reach him."

"I'll do what I can. I'll ask him to join the Christian Action Core. It's a group that has a lot of pastoral exposure to New York. I'll try getting him involved."

So it began. Richard did join the Core and used his skill on the guitar to play for rallies, retreats, and school liturgies. His trip to France was crucial in launching his career as a multilinguist, and he used his languages in his later practice of law. In gratitude, the doctor and his wife included me in their weekend excursions. I met them at their home in Bay Ridge and sat with Gabe in the living room as we awaited Grace's appearance at the top of the staircase. It was a ritual repeated each time.

"You know, Rock," Gabe said, "Grace and I started dating at Fordham when we were almost twenty. I knew she was the one, and I never questioned my choice. We're quite a match. She's given me two bright kids, Gabby and Richard. My son can be difficult, but he'll find his way. Choosing is tricky even when you're a doctor."

"How do you mean?" I asked.

"Rock, half my clients are women who sometimes want to pay with more than money. It's flattering, but I'd never jeopardize my relationship with Grace. She's every woman to me. Anyhow, I'm fussy where I put my penis."

I blushed scarlet, but Gabe missed my embarrassment. He was too busy watching Grace descend the staircase in her Emilio Pucci dress. A swirl of asymmetric colors, it perfectly suited her sinuous frame. Her shoulder length hair and radiant smile prompted a déjà vu of my aunt Rita. Presently, Gabe, Grace, and I would dine at a classic restaurant and then visit a cabaret after. I never saw money or plastic exchanged. We rose from the table and left. Somehow the bill got paid. Was it done by mailed check, or had Gabe given his card numbers in advance? I never learned his method, but I've since imitated his manner.

When I returned from France the following summer, I brought back the perfume Prince Rainier had commissioned for his wife, Grace Kelly. It was called "Grace." It was available only in Monaco. *What an achievement,* I thought, *to buy the doctor's wife something she could not acquire in the United States.* I still see her opening the box, removing the flacon, and testing the scent on her wrist, first looking at the name and then at me. Lifting her arm in my direction, she said, "Rock, smell me." She spoke with such pleasure that it superseded the overt thanks she might have given. Gratitude was implied in the satisfaction.

I lost contact with the Cucolos during my graduate study at Harvard, though I did return for Gabby's church wedding where I preached the homily. Shortly after, Gabe and Grace came to my ordination, and I still have pictures of them kneeling to receive my first blessing. I never guessed that two years later I would solace Grace. Gabe had died of a massive heart attack.

"Rock," she said, as we sat in a room away from the parlor where Gabe was waked, "I'm angry at that bloke in there."

"Angry?" I said, for she had never been angry at Gabe in her life.

"Yes, angry. He and I had a pact. We spoke of a common disaster. We thought it might happen in a plane crash since we traveled together. He didn't keep his promise. The son of a bitch went and left without me."

Now she is in her eighties. Grace never remarried though men had tried courting her. Nothing ever came of their wife-wooing. How could it?

She cherished Gabe till the end and still does. In her person, the psalmist proved right: Love is stronger than death.

I have the same rapprochement with other couples for whom I played the man at one side; the husband was at the other while the wife sat between us. Snippets of conversation come to mind.

I remember Bob and Nancy, and their daughter, Alexandra, who said to her father, a famous church architect: "Dad, do you see where Mother is? She's surrounded by men. Aren't you jealous?"

"On the contrary, Alexandra, I see how lucky I am. Your mother can have as many vertical relationships as she wants provided they don't get horizontal."

I remember John and Véronique, friends during the Harvard years, and the evening meals when Véronique prepared stuffed eggplant and shelled peas with warm cream, and then capped the dinner with apple tart. I often brought a *grand cru* Bordeaux, and we three finished our wine watching a film with Véronique sitting cross-legged between John and me: shades of Trouffaut's *Jules and Jim.*

In recent memory MaryLou and Joseph Peters stand out, sharp and clear. I met them at the Westin Resort on St. John in the U.S. Virgin Islands. I was sitting at Mango's, the hotel's outdoor café, correcting the galleys of a novel. I'm fond of Mango's, especially the front table; there I can inhale the scented breezes, feel the unbroken sun, and hear Portuguese *fado* piped through the speakers. My first experience sitting there introduced me to MaryLou and JP. Here is my account. MaryLou's is more factual while mine invokes authorial license.

I looked up briefly from the galleys, my eyes weary from print. The deli stood directly in front. I decided to interrupt my work, buy myself a sandwich, and retrieve my table. I always find eating *alfresco* restorative.

I espied a slender woman in a broad sun hat, dark glasses, and a summer chemise. A tall, distinguished gentleman followed her. He resembled Hubert de Givenchy while she recalled Rosalind Russell in looks and stature. Noticing that on his tray was a tuna salad sandwich, I reacted:

"That's exactly what I want."

"Order it and then come and join us," said the unnamed woman.

Presently I returned with my sandwich and joined them. I've been joining them ever since: at their Maryland estate, at their villa on St. John, on an island-hopping sailboat; and all because of tuna and an engrossing exchange in which I learned we held in common persons, places, and things. They were graduates of Catholic colleges to which they were devoted.

After ten minutes of conversation with MaryLou and JP, she suddenly asked, "Are you a priest?" The question sprang from her intuitive insight to which I have since become accustomed. I answered affirmatively. Another question followed:

"Are you a Jesuit?"

It took poise to manage my astonishment.

"That's my background," I said without finessing my words, for nuances would come later. "I teach comparative religion and courses in Buddhism. I'm currently proofing a novel."

A three-hour conversation, sparked by my mix of vocations, sealed our friendship. I have since delivered a homily at their wedding, baptized one grandchild, and unwittingly given first communion to another. I'm their peripatetic chaplain who celebrates Mass for their island guests. The Sunday liturgy is followed by a delicious brunch. Both happen in February. I've performed my *Gospel Limerick* in their villa turned cabaret for the night, and I have hosted them for dinner in New York. I've sat with them for theater at Lincoln Center, and heard MaryLou exclaim, "I like being between my two Josephs."

"So what's your sexual thing?" asks a brash New Yorker, assuming that by naming my arousal pattern the question is addressed.

"Trisexual," I reply. "I'm keen on couples. Their commitment attracts me."

"What accounts for this? The word *trisexual* isn't even in Webster's."

"It's reparative. As my parents aged, they grew apart. They conducted their lives in an emotional stalemate like beloved enemies. My father could not keep pace with my mother's spacious intelligence or her Martella temper. He might have done better with a hausfrau. Still, they never separated or divorced. She cared for him during his seven year bout with illness. She never sequestered him in a nursing home. He stayed in his own room in his own bed after medical protocols failed. When finally he was rushed to the hospital, the last word on his lips before he expired was 'Lucie.'

"My brother took pictures of my father in the last weeks of his life. They are deeply affecting. Like a Christian in the coliseum he endured his martyrdom without complaint. Both my parents were models of dying. They accepted its arrival as a matter of course without resistance or acquiescence. It was the last thing they did, so they determined to do it well without fuss or fanfare but with dignity."

A student friend who is interested in being a fiction writer invited me to coffee. He had read my short stories and asked me for a novel. He planned a trip home for the holidays and wanted, so he said, to have me accompany him. As we sat at Starbuck's, I dutifully inscribed *The Devil's Interval*: "To Benjamin in friendship, more than yesterday but less than tomorrow." My dedication liberated a flood of questions. I replied with candor; caffeine has a way of loosening my tongue. He moved from literary interests to those engaging my life. What we said to each other I present as a dialogue. Call it "Bucking Stars at Starbuck's."

Benjamin: After seven novels, two plays, two collections of short stories, a memoir, and a new novel in the works, how do you know you're growing as a novelist?

Joseph: I'm more preoccupied with style than with content. My aim is a lucid, polished prose characterized by terse expression that sacrifices neither cadence nor euphony. Together they make up the great embalmer along with irony to pique interest and wit to induce a smile. These qualities may produce what every serious writer wants, namely, a classic; something that stays ahead of its time by aspiring to permanence. The text remains fresh without being faddish and continues to give pleasure.

Another sign of growth for a male writer is to present women as complete persons; to be so successful in expressing their mental and emotional states that women reading the text take the author for a woman. It's doing for one's story what Tolstoy did for *Anna Karenina*: creating a female character in the round. If I demonstrate such growth in any way, I owe it to women like Maureen McCafferty and Joanna Datillo who have been lifelong friends. *Portrait of a Woman* and *The Devil's Interval* are dedicated to them in gratitude. In each instance, *eros* and *agape* have combined to produce an intimacy that is binding yet conjugally free. In characterizing these relationships, I'm tempted to join the Greek words and speak of *agaperos*. But the neologism advances nothing and succeeds in being more clever than clarifying.

Benjamin: Is writing what gives you joy?

Joseph: Yes. When my imagination and the flow of words coincide, I'm euphoric. In a serene setting with no uncouth intrusion of technology, I exercise total concentration; it's there I feel closest to the beatific vision this side of paradise. It's as pleasurable as dining with a cherished friend.

Benjamin: What for you are signs of literary success?

Joseph: That my books are in print and being read by an audience known for its literacy. I prefer them on college reading lists where they bridge both sacred and secular worlds. While I hope they will instruct, they are meant to entertain. I have no dogmatic axe to grind and no wish to proselytize. I'm simply alerting readers to a depth dimension that is theirs by birthright. A more overt sign of success would be to view my stories as films. I would happily imitate Somerset Maugham's cinematic versions of

The Painted Veil and *The Razor's Edge,* or of his short stories, "Rain" and "The Letter."

Benjamin: What do you want as your legacy?

Joseph: Peering down from my celestial perch, I would be pleased to see uniform editions of my books on the shelves of Harvard, Oxford, or any institution passing critical scrutiny. My pleasure would be enhanced if my books sat on the night tables of the pope or the president.

Benjamin: How do you imagine your later years, what is tactfully called the end of your life?

Joseph: I see myself on monastic grounds close to nature—but not remote from an urban center—in trekking distance of Gregorian chant, and practicing calligraphy as the sun rises or sets. My room will be simple without being charmless. Japanese design accomplishes both admirably.

Benjamin: How do you imagine your death?

Joseph: Within earshot of monks chanting the *Memorare,* the scent of *Joy* on my pillow, and loving faces alongside.

Benjamin: How to you want to be remembered?

Joseph: As a good friend and an informed priest: witty and urbane, thoughtful and funny; companionable in the way a deceased friend once remarked: "Joseph, I can take you anywhere."

Benjamin: And an epitaph? What words should be cut on your tombstone?

Joseph: I want Latin for my final rejoinder: "Quia bene vixit, propterea bene scripsit." "Because he lived well, he therefore wrote well."

As I finish this chronicle, I'm fully aware that I've left my reader pondering words on a tombstone. I've run through my memoir to see if I could somehow fabricate a brighter ending. I'm startled to learn that without any planning I've written a buoyant commentary on the doctrine of providence. For something quite surprising has resulted from the drama in which I unwittingly played my part:

> From my infantile caregivers: unconditional trust in human diversity;
> From the Jesuits: humanism profound both in range and concentration;
> From the Harvard faculty: appreciation of faith in its global context;
> From my Buddhist mentors: Zen enlightenment enriching the Gospel;
> From an unmarried priesthood: artistic freedom to create spiritual thrillers.

Skeptics may be scornful of my writing because of its religious resonance, but the believing public trusts in divine guidance to sway human events. What looks like coincidence they know is providence acting anonymously. So this memoir is not that surprising after all.

Appendix I

The Fourth Letter

(for PDH)

Once a week, when he was near Gramercy Park, Julian Lazare visited the home of Marcus Hoffmann, his former professor of comparative scripture. Marcus, who had just turned eighty, was university lecturer at several prestigious institutions: Louvain, Oxford, and Cambridge. He had recently received an honorary degree from Harvard with the publication of his thirtieth book. The champagne Julian carried was to celebrate the event and offer another occasion for gratitude. Because of Hoffmann's intervention twenty-five years earlier, Julian had pursued a doctorate in classical languages. His eminence in the field had earned him the title of Hoffmann's protégé. How Marcus and Julian first met had become anecdotal.

"You seem to be having trouble translating."

Marcus had stopped by Julian's café table after he noticed a Latin dictionary. The younger man was puzzling over a line from Cicero. Julian's Latin was self-taught, but without classroom repetition his memory of the five declensions was shaky.

"You're not construing the noun correctly. It's not in the nominative case but the ablative."

"How can you tell?"

"From a lifetime of reading. The ablative ending has a long 'a.'" Marcus reached into his wallet.

"Here's my card. If eleven at night isn't too late, call me with problems."

"Call you?"

"We can handle them over the phone. That's how I learned Sanskrit."

Soon a tutorial at the café began for three hours a week and continued for a year. Marcus then introduced Julian to Greek. What resulted was a mastery that earned him a scholarship to Harvard's program in classics and a PhD with the highest honors. Julian's academic career he owed to Marcus whom he called *praecursor:* the forerunner.

He often visited Marcus's garden apartment to assure himself the older man's health had improved. During the past year, Marcus survived a severe bout of illness. An aneurism of the brain had induced painful migraines, and when the malady was diagnosed, he underwent surgery. Whenever weather permitted, he and Julian sat on the patio enjoying tea and scones, which Marcus said had quickened his recovery. Today by exception champagne accompanied their scones. Julian had finished toasting Marcus's latest honor and then added, "I thought you might find this cartoon funny. It's from *The New Yorker*. Since you don't have your glasses, I'll read it to you."

He held it up for viewing. The sketch was clear: a papyrus trailed on the ground while a scribe wrote at a table. He looked like John the Evangelist on Patmos finishing the Fourth Gospel. Standing alongside the papyrus, John's secretary was saying: "Quit worrying about corroborating your sources—it's not as if anyone's going to take this literally."

Marcus and Julian laughed.

"I thought you'd be amused," Julian said. "It's typical of *The New Yorker* to poke fun at agnosticism while supporting it."

"Your cartoon, Julian, reminds me of something else. A dabbler in religion left it. He claimed to know more about Jesus than the early church. He said he owed his knowledge to John."

Pausing thoughtfully, Marcus asked, "Do you recall, Julian, how the Fourth Gospel ends?"

"Yes, I've read it many times."

"Would you recite it aloud?"

"It goes something like this: 'There are many other things Jesus did. If they were all set down, one by one, I suppose the whole world could not contain the books that would need to be written.'"

"Have you ever wondered about those 'other things'? Are they miracles or aftershocks? Whatever they are, they're not in John's Gospel. Where are they? Were they recorded in a later epistle?"

"You know as well as I, Marcus, we have three accepted as canonical."

"Julian, go to the last shelf on my bookcase and remove the box. Yes, that one. Bring it here. Pull your chair over to inspect the contents."

Seated beside Marcus, Julian opened the box and removed photocopies of a papyrus. A translation in colloquial English alternated with pages of Greek.

"Read the title," Marcus said.

"*The Fourth Letter of John.*"

Julian looked at Marcus for help, but receiving none returned to the document. Curiosity pressed him to page through the text. Occasionally, he stopped to check a paragraph.

"From a cursory look I'd say it resembles John's letters in content and style. The Greek receive a Hebrew turn, but it's lost in the English version that borders on slang. It could be the translator's effort to return the reader to the original. It feels authentic, but it's an imitation; in fact, a forgery."

"But why would anyone go to such lengths? To write an epistle likely to be judged a fake—what's the point?"

"I haven't a clue."

"Julian, take the document home. See what you think and then return in a week. We'll compare notes the way we puzzled over Plato."

"More serious fun. That's what you called our tutorials."

"They're the only ones worth remembering."

When Julian arrived home, he wasted no time in examining the papyrus. His knowledge of Greek made the textual reading swift. What focused his attention was the translation. The colloquial version was exaggerated in contrast to the original composed with sobriety. The letter invited excess for it contained overheated passages. Originally written as third person narratives, the translator had translated them as monologues to heighten the drama. They claimed accuracy from conversations with Mary with whom John had lived on Ephesus. The speakers were beneficiaries for whom Jesus had performed miracles like Lazarus or the couple at Cana; others like the Samaritan woman or Thomas claimed a conversion by faith. What they shared in common was an urge to relate their meeting with Christ, and how he had changed their lives. Contrary to piety, the outcome did not go well. The stories were notable not for peace, but a conflict that oscillated between nature and grace ending in exhaustion. Julian read the epistle as if his life depended on it:

The Fourth Letter of John

Introduction

From John the Elder to Marcian whom I cherish:

I have so much to tell you I'd hoped to visit you in person. But I have to do it with pen and ink, since I can't leave the local church. You've asked me about the "other things," which I mentioned at the end of my gospel. I pass them on just as I heard them from those chosen for the Lord's intervention. I'm reporting their stories, so you may grow in faith and your joy will be full.

I've also drawn them from conversations with his mother Mary, who became my own at the foot of the cross. She will help you realize her son's promise: to have eternal life.

My dear friend, nothing makes me happier than to see a follower cling to the truth against all odds. May these stories persuade you that whoever struggles to believe belongs to God.

Cana

"My wife and I are celebrating an anniversary. It's not our marital vows, but the embarrassment saved us by a guest. It was explained by the servants after the company went home.

"During the wedding something went wrong. Anxiety was on the servants' faces, not to mention, the sommelier's. I ascribed it to the numerous guests and the heightened demand for wine. Neither my wife nor I realized that's where the problem lay. The caterers had run short. Cocktail trays made their rounds along with the hors d'oeuvres, but there were fewer glasses.

"I glanced at a woman speaking to a man who may have been a relation. He listened, but when he didn't act, she took the initiative to call the servers over. I turned back to my wife's family. My in-laws were everywhere. Suddenly the trays made the rounds and wine was being liberally dispensed. People began asking for seconds and thirds. I took the time to sample some myself. It was superlative, a pinot noir layered with raspberry and truffles. I don't recall it during pre-prandials, and to keep such a vintage till the end is exceptional. No one complained at the reverse order and neither did I. But the wine steward looked puzzled.

"So here we are, recalling that memorable wine. If only I could find it. But a season in which sun and soil perfectly consort with the grape is miraculous. How can I return to jug wine when that Cana vintage teases my palate? My wife says it's odd to clink an empty glass, but I'd rather go without and quaff a memory.

"To a stranger I owe this abstinence from drink, for he made the best the enemy of what's good. I now search for excellence everywhere and swallow my disappointment."

The Samaritan Woman

"It began with a meeting at a well and a request for water. He knew I was a Samaritan, but it didn't stop this Jew from asking. It was an excuse to talk intimately.

"In exchange he offered me living water. I asked myself if this was a new cocktail. He said it was a thirst quencher. Suddenly I caught on. He was talking about my insatiable need for men. He guessed the number five and was right about the sixth, a retainer whom I haven't bothered to wed.

"How did this Jew read me so well? Ashamed at exposure, I changed the subject. I blurted out something about hope for a redeemer. I might have said knight in shining armor, given my Cinderella complex. I meant someone empowered to do good. The current jargon is savior. It's then he got really intimate. He settled on savior and announced it was him. My face dropped along with the jug I carried. Something told me he spoke the truth. I had to get away, so I ran into town like a mad woman. I had to share the news. Instead of writing me off, I got a hearing from the townspeople. What it did to them I can't say. What it's done to me is clear.

"It's been a disaster. Nothing before his coming prepared me for what followed. I'm the same outsider to the Jews, but now I'm *persona non grata* among my own. (Thank you, Jesus.) It's one thing to say that the savior has come, another that he's from the Jews. Now I'm shunned in both quarters. As for men, even when I spend time with them, I can't hold my interest longer than overnight. They're in and out, so to speak. Why tolerate a bore who's a few faculties posing as a man? I've met the real thing. Sensitive, good-looking, strong but tender. His origin must be impressive: like father like son.

"You meet a man like that once if you're lucky. Measured against him, those who've preceded and followed are forgettable. I'd rather live alone. (Thank you, Jesus.) My apartment rings with silence, the only thing keeping me company. I go to bed with it and wake up with it. When I break my silence—Jacob's well is still the place to hook up—I recall his words and the interest leaves me. That's what comes of meeting someone with a messiah complex that turns out to be real.

"I used to think something is better than nothing. Now nothing is better than anything. Why did I go out that day? Why did I drink with a perfect stranger? Why, Jesus, didn't you leave 'well' enough alone?"

The Official's Son

"He was all I had. We were a family of two for I lost the boy's mother at childbirth. Though I managed with local support to raise him, it wasn't easy. Always fragile as an infant, he inherited his mother's vulnerability.

"It was difficult adjusting to official obligations. My role as liaison officer to the procurator meant hiring Jewish help. They were as loath to deal with my paganism as I with their sectarianism. My son's winning ways eased hostility. He's an enchanting boy and appealingly handsome. I thank my wife for qualities which in her absence live on in him.

"As I've said he was frail and subject to chronic illness. Periodically his lungs filled and coughing shook his frame as he tried to dislodge the mucus. His wheezing was constant as he reached for breath. What most boys took for granted—running and playing—was for him a rare experience. He spent hours indoors with mustard plasters on his back, listening to his friends playing in the street. Always ready when the fevers came and his temperature spiked, we went from warm compresses to alcohol baths.

"Bronchial infection occurred with calculable regularity followed by the pulmonary ritual until his health returned. We celebrated with a trip to Egypt, for my son never tired of seeing pyramids, placing offerings in the temple of Giza, or gazing in astonishment at the sphinx.

"This year his illness returned predictably. We thought the medications would prove effective. Nothing worked. The cough grew louder, his temperature higher, and the gasping more laborious. My son was burning up. Baths offered relief, but the fever would not budge. Though the servants redoubled their prayers to the Penates, the household gods did not respond. I began a novena to the god of health, Asclepius, offering him flowers and incense. My pleas went unheeded. While the illness waxed and waned, my son held on by threads. He was nearing the end.

"It was then that his nanny, a Judean woman, spoke of the man in Galilee. 'They claim he works miracles,' she said without specifics. I assumed healing was one of them, so I asked her. 'I don't know,' she replied, 'but I heard at Cana he saved newlyweds from embarrassment. His kindness may extend to children.' Meeting him became mandatory.

"It's been weeks since that encounter, and what I call his one o'clock wonder. That's when the fever broke and my son fell into restorative sleep. I keep hearing the words, 'your son will live,' and ask myself if it was an isolated instance. Must I schedule an annual trip to ensure my son's healing? I should have asked for a lifetime of health and locked in the miracle. All I do now is wait till next year and hope.

"While I'm drawn to this Jewish miracle worker, I object to his tribal deity. I have not evicted Asclepius from his niche, for doubts have me thinking that I need all the gods I can get."

The Paralytic

"Have you ever imagined living at ground level? Squatting day after day looking up for help? That's how I led my life. I competed for compassion with the blind and lame around me. But they were ambulatory. Paralysis from the waist down confined me to the use of arms and hands. Legs and feet dangled like streamers in the wind. For thirty-eight years I lived as half a man.

"I tried to reach the pool near the Sheep Gate. Only when the waters stirred was a cure guaranteed. Those waiting on the porch arrived first. They moved at a clip while I never matched their speed. Every day I dealt with disappointment. Immobility confined me till he happened by—I mean the miracle worker. He must have watched my frustration. Sidling near, he asked, 'Do you want to get well?'

"I looked up. He was tall, lean, with swarthy good looks. His words were arrows out of a quiver. I told him how powerless I was to reach the pool before the others. He did not pity my plight but said, 'Rise, take up your mat and walk.'

"I didn't question the command. Four decades of muscular damage challenged his words, but I did what he enjoined. Suddenly the shock set in that I was standing. My brain empowered my legs and I walked. I imagined running with the wind in my face, diving into a wave and swimming, feeling arousal as I drew near women—all because he charged me to get up. So began my risen life.

"I cannot describe my joy standing at full height. I spun around, squatted once or twice, and kicked out my legs. Everything worked. What was blocking the sun was a collision with priests who bristled at my cure. They asked for the culprit's name, but I was ignorant. I learned it later while offering thanks in the temple. He happened by.

"'You're well,' he said and then warned, 'don't sin or something worse will happen.'

"I asked myself what he meant. What could be worse than *rigor mortis* from the waist down? I got my answer. He foresaw the fantasies of thirty-eight years, and how bent I was on testing them. I'm compensating for decades of paralysis. Life is a game of seduction, the 'something worse' he said would befall me. 'So many women, so little time' is my mantra. I used to live immobilized on the ground. Now desire stops me. Twice in my lifetime I've been stuck. I'm desperate for a risen life in which I'm not just up but upright. So I descend to the pool at the Sheep Gate and enter the waters whenever they stir. I pray they'll reverse his miracle and free me."

The Adulteress

"Neither will I condemn you," he told me, and then added, "Go and sin no more." It was more easily said than done. He might as well have counseled, "Go and work no more. Go find yourself another profession. At this stage in life? How do I support myself? I still have a pretty figure. I look younger than I am. I know how to give myself, so a man finds a little happiness. That's what I do best.

"But go and sin no more? Impossible. It's not that I haven't tried. I've let myself stop and take a break now and then. But he said 'no more' and that's a lifetime. When it's worked, it's because I have that scene in front of me.

"I'm crouching in a corner wrapped in a bedsheet. Men leering at me have rocks in their hands while they flex their wrists. It's me splayed against the wall and not the man I slept with. He went scot-free and slipped into the crowd. He's also holding a rock.

"I hear Jesus's challenge, 'if one of you is without sin.' Holding my breath, I wait for the shower of stone. Nothing. Then I watch him write in the dust. Is it my imagination or do I see words? Robber, perjurer, murderer, fornicator—the list goes on as the rocks drop and only the two of us remain. He does not rebuke but enjoins me not to sin.

"Did he know to what he condemned me? Did he realize his compassion had so unhinged me that when I sell myself for shekels my mind is elsewhere? I don't want what my body intends. Is that the same as not sinning? It's the best I can do. When I'm old and faded and please no more I'll heed his words. Till then, Jesus, make me chaste but not yet."

The Man Born Blind

"As a child, I recall a chink of light and darkness closing in. Current opinion held it was the result of my sin or my parents'. He didn't view it that way, I mean the wonder worker. He intervened with a makeshift medicine. He made a salve of dirt and spittle and bade me wash in the Pool of Siloam. My eyes opened. Whenever asked, I say my vision was mud-born.

"My cure was the talk of the town. Gossip caught the ears of the rabbis who, using the same tactics with the paralytic, threatened me because of my Sabbath cure. After being barraged about how, when, and where, I asked them, 'Why? Do you want to follow him?' They were enraged at the idea they would follow a sinner. I replied, 'Nobody's heard of a person restoring sight unless he's from God.' They resented being lectured, so I was expelled from temple and family. Talk about a double whammy.

"Later, he sought me out and invited my faith. With nothing to lose and gratitude to give I accepted him as Lord.

"It's been months since my sight was restored, and my eyes have never been sharper. In another age, I might have heard: 'Perfect. They're twenty-twenty.' So why not rejoice over access to light? Why resent this vision? When I observe the Roman world around me, how conquest creates famine, disease, and hatred, I'm nostalgic for blindness. I recall feeling safe under cover of darkness. Now with full vision I grope."

Lazarus

"He brought me back to life to please my sisters, Martha especially. With him she adopted that tone which always turned me off. I can see her point though, for he stayed away till I decomposed. When he finally arrived and Mary's rebuke followed Martha's, what could he do? He brought me back from the dead.

"It was a rehearsal for his reappearance after three days in a tomb. My exit from that crypt made him a sensation. But no one asked if I wanted to be revived. Resuscitation is not resurrection. It means a replay of the whole rigmarole: illness, collapse of organs, death rattle, and letting go. Once was enough. But to endure it again?

"For that repeat performance I have him to thank. Knowing what to expect fills me with dread. How I wish he'd left well enough alone. I was adjusting nicely when I awoke on hearing my name. Since then, I'm a dead man walking."

Thomas

"I was out when they said he came. Trapped in that upper room, I was suffering cabin fever. At night we lay there, cheek by jowl, fearful of the Jews. A beard disguised me. So I slipped from the house down a back alley. That's how I missed him.

"I walked for hours replaying how he went about doing good. In the end death was stronger. Without power to back his goodness, his story read like a tragedy. The flaw was his pride of origin. Despite so-called divinity, it had no cash value. I wasn't there at Calvary—John was—but crucifixion was the clincher. Talk about barking up the wrong tree. With Roman legions everywhere, he needed power to succeed. Pacifism got him nowhere.

"Such were my thoughts as I wandered the back streets, angry at being duped. Three years a disciple and what did I have to show? No wife or family, no career: all of it sacrificed to charisma and a preaching, holding me spellbound.

"When I finally got home, a chorus of voices greeted me: 'We've seen him.' I was in no mood for group hallucination. I know how hysteria takes over. It's like new wine bubbling in old casks. Unmoved by their account, I replied, 'when you're dead, you're dead. Nails and spear were conclusive.'

"One thing changed my mind. Call it my wild card. I wanted to prove by touch what they'd witnessed: to truck up close and feel it. They kept saying, 'We've seen him,' and I said, 'Happy are those who haven't seen and needn't believe.' We reached a dead end: their faith against my disbelief. I refused to be taken in. Correction: I wanted to be taken in, to have my finger probe the imprint of nails and my hand the hollow of his side. I announced it. It was an impossible demand asking for tactile proof. But I'm a Mediterranean male, and if I can't feel it, I don't know it. It horrified them. All they could do was protest.

"So things stood. I was again gagging from closeness shut up indoors. I planned once more to escape when the shutters flew open. The door came unbolted as if a wind had slipped back the latch.

"There he was.

"He walked into the circle of brethren and over to me. No one asked, 'Who is it?' Greeting me with shalom, he addressed my demands.

"'Thomas,' he said, 'place your finger here and your hand there.'

"I hesitated, but he repeated to position my finger and hand. The intimacy he invited was shocking, but I obeyed. Who among you has ever probed a resurrected body? Even Magdalene was told not to touch. Here in full view of his wounds I was reaching for them. No airbrushing but the real thing.

"The contact was a lightning bolt. It shook me while the pressure brought me to my knees, and then the words, for he never stopped teaching: 'Blessed are those who without seeing believe.' He might have said, 'Without touching.'

"For years I've carried that contact scene. My words as I knelt there, calling him Lord and God, never changed history. My name is still paired with doubt. I'm the patron saint of skeptics and borderline believers. The best they can say is, 'Help me to want to want believing.' They hanker for faith. Some never get much farther.

"While wandering in India, I offered as witness my renunciation. I punished touch to atone for my disbelief. I went without sex and food, water and lodging. My clothes became rags and the ground my bed.

"Some people asked me, 'Thomas, are you sure it happened? Were you really in touch?' My senses are so dim now I scarcely hear them. I barely can see while taste and smell are diminished. Nothing remains for me but a scene of genuflection, and that beautiful upright posture of a free man as he kneels."

The Purpose of This Letter

Marcian, I have so much more to tell you that I would rather dispense with paper and speak with you directly. For now let these stories reveal how the Lord dealt with disciples in ways other than miraculous. I share them so that by keeping faith in the Son of God you may find life in his name. Peace be with you.

A week after receiving "The Fourth Letter," Julian visited Marcus's apartment. Again the mild temperature invited them outdoors. They were seated on the patio while copies of the text lay open.

"I'm glad we met this afternoon," Julian said. "It will be weeks before we see each other. I leave for Rome tonight and tomorrow I start work at Hadrian's Villa. I'm excavating the temple of Antinous. It's part of the villa and recently discovered."

Marcus was more eager to hear Julian's reaction to the letter.

"So what made our forger produce this deception?"

Julian had anticipated the question. He knew Marcus's rigor for focusing an issue and was ready with a reply.

"Fanaticism pressed into piety. It comes from an imagination driven by misguided faith. It's well-intentioned and moving. The fervor doesn't keep the letter from being delusional. Theologians might wink and look away. Freud would have pounced."

Marcus did not answer, so Julian broke the silence.

"What are you thinking?"

"My opinion is more generous. I'm using a norm other than authenticity. The epistle is saying that if you think involvement with Jesus promoted happiness, you've got it wrong. It led to lives of exertion and failure, of renewal followed by defeat. How else could God's mercy triumph . . . Julian, the look on your face is disapproval."

"The monologues are gripping. I'll allow for the slang that keeps them honest. You're forced to face the cost of discipleship. But that's different from claiming the text is genuine. Are you defending forgery?"

"Yes, but not as forgery."

"Then how?"

"As art. I enjoy the reversal at the end of each speech. The mood swings belong to this decade. They're cautious and committed. The text isn't reverent but shows how Jesus falls short. Despite his personality, he's left with failures that nearly succeeded. He's not surprised, for he knows something is stronger than grace."

"What's that?"

"Freedom and its ability to thwart. Something else bolsters the letter. Jesus' followers hanker for their lives before conversion. Without them they're at a loss. It reminds me of what I've learned about myself. If Christianity makes me moral, it doesn't make me content. I might have been happier as a Greek with gods as ideals. It would have been easier living in an age that pursued power and celebrity—all the perks of Olympus."

"That's the writer's viewpoint. Surely you don't agree. You're known for hugging the shoreline of a text. This version strays into choppy water. It's not scholarship. Still, I'd like to meet the author."

"You're speaking to him."

Julian's face collapsed in disbelief, then rallied.

"You said a dabbler in religion left you the letter. That hardly applies to you."

"Whoever writes about the sacred is a dabbler. The exceptions are insiders like the founders of great religions. Jesus was the supreme insider. You and I remain outside dabbling with words."

"Did you write the Greek text too?"

"Yes. It was composed first and then the English."

"Why go to such lengths?"

"That's the question I asked before we parted."

"Do you know the answer?"

"May I appeal to Buddhism?"

"I always find what you say appealing."

Marcus smiled and continued, "Centuries after Buddha's death new scriptures were composed. They begin with the stock expression, 'Thus have I heard' that the Buddha did this or that in such and such a place. The point being made is that here is an eyewitnesses account of what happened. The historical Buddha was already dead for several centuries. To what Buddha then are the texts referring? Not the one known as Siddhartha who roamed the Ganges.

"Mahayana, as these scriptures were called, strove for a wider interpretation. The texts addressed new circumstances. This is how we have believed, they seemed to say, but how shall we believe? They offer a more inclusive vision. 'The Fourth Letter' does the same by expanding the Gospel to meet a reluctant age."

"But Marcus, why go to such lengths? John has Jesus confronting skeptics all the time. He accuses them with the words, 'O you of little faith.'"

"We're not just dealing with skepticism. Now it's communication. It's crisscrossing e-mails and cell phones, text messaging and iPods, CDs, and DVDs, not to mention movies, radio, and TV. How can the Gospel be heard above this Babel? To be effective, it needs to jump from the page: to dramatize how the Cana newlyweds coped. How the Samaritan woman, the adulteress, the paralytic, and the blind man—not to mention Thomas—muddled through. What befell them happens to us because their story is ours. We play their roles. 'The Fourth Letter' may not be part of the scriptural canon, but it's semi-canonical; it's revelatory like any literary text."

"You know what your colleagues will say, Marcus. You've gone off the deep end. Why risk so much?"

"With more honorary degrees than time remaining, I'm at an age when health is a gift. Like Thomas I need to be touched. I yearn for living words to saturate me. Nothing shallow in drips and drabs. I want immersion. If I can't find it, I'll do it for myself and for you too."

"For me?"

"You're the heir apparent. Years ago, Julian, I didn't stop at your café table just to encourage a PhD. True, you've used your mind for scholarship, but you require one thing more for genius."

"What?"

"Imagination. That's how the universe got launched. Divine energy sparked the image that galvanized matter. Artists have followed suit by using marble and music, pigment, and poetry and scripture. What they create springs from the same impulse."

"So 'The Fourth Letter' is inspired?"

"Yes. It's the school of John, but the letter heightens what he said. Authority resides in the words."

"How can you tell?"

"On hearing the text, you become empowered. You're lost in the overlap."

"Lost in the overlap"—the words repeated themselves on the plane to Rome and at odd times through his week. Julian was feeling a connection with Hadrian who had overlapped, not with a text, but with his lover Antinous dead from suicide. Hadrian's grief was so intense that it prompted statues and temples, coins and a cult; finally, it built a city. Any effort to ease the emperor's bereavement was met with resistance. Hadrian's bond with Antinous was total while his depression remained irreversible. *It was an overlap,* Julian thought, *he could do without.*

It happened during the second week of excavating. Julian received a phone call telling him Marcus had suffered a stroke. While arranging with Alitalia for a flight home, he learned Marcus had slipped into a coma and died. When Julian arrived at his New York apartment, a letter awaited him from Marcus's lawyer, James Cosgrove: "You have been named Prof. Hoffmann's sole heir," he wrote. "Although his books will go to Widener Library, the town house, bank account, and classical artifacts are left to you. I will execute the will this month. Meanwhile, Marcus's colleagues have asked you to deliver the eulogy at Memorial Chapel, Harvard Yard the day after tomorrow. It's scheduled for 9:00 a.m. during the morning service. A reception will follow. I'm leaving you my address and phone number, should you have any questions."

Julian took advantage of the number and called the lawyer.

"Mr. Cosgrove, this is Julian Lazare. I'm settling back into my apartment after returning from Rome. I read your letter and need some clarity."

"How can I help you, Dr. Lazare?"

"Have I understood you correctly that Prof. Hoffmann's eulogy is slated for the morning service at Mem Chapel?"

"Yes."

"But the service is restricted to fifteen minutes. Why did Marcus's friends schedule it for so short a period? The time slot is unreasonable. Marcus had a rich career. To address it in a quarter of an hour is not possible."

"I understand your concern, Dr. Lazare. Your reaction was mine. It was not his colleagues who decided the time. It was Marcus."

"But why?"

"He wanted to avoid adulation. While Marcus was alive, he had a low tolerance for awards. 'They come with the territory,' he once said, but he shunned fanfare. A fifteen minute tribute is in character."

Julian put the phone down and sank in his chair. A quarter of an hour to acknowledge a life, that's all he had. He picked up his attaché case, left the apartment, and walked over to Gramercy Park. He still had Marcus's house key to let himself in. He entered the foyer and walked through the rooms to the garden terrace. Opening the screen door, he sat down at the patio table and surveyed the artfully arranged plot of land: the rose and azalea bushes were in bloom while a twenty-foot oak still cast its protective shadow. The calm was palpable. He sat there imagining Marcus across from him. He recalled how they often said nothing while enjoying the peace.

Once during a long silence Marcus interrupted the stillness, "While the best amenity is outward serenity, I prefer the civility of inner tranquility."

"Do you do that often?"

"Do what?"

"Break into rhyme."

"You know, Julian, that's an enchanting question. Yes, it's happened a lot lately. I find myself playing with verse."

"Sounds like a talent recently discovered. What prompts it?"

"A heightened ability that comes with senility."

As Julian sat there, the anecdotes multiplied. Removing pad and pen from his attaché case, he began to write. *What better place*, he thought, *than this corner to encompass a life.*

Two days later he took a seven o'clock flight to Boston, hailed a cab outside of Logan Airport, and drove along the Charles River toward Harvard Square. The traffic slowed his arrival. He reached the gates of the yard, walked past John Harvard's statue, then up the steps into the chapel. He was escorted to his seat on the chancel before a packed congregation. No introduction was needed: Julian featured prominently in the memorial booklet.

After a short hymn he stepped to the podium. He looked out on an expanse of faces. Colleagues, dignitaries, faculty, and students had flown or driven in from Cambridge, the country, and around the world. Julian began in Latin:

"'*Consummavit multum in brevi tempore,*' the psalmist tells us. 'In a brief career he accomplished much.' This morning, I'm altering the Latin to respect Prof. Hoffmann's incomparable life. '*Consummavit maximum in longo tempore*': 'In a long career he achieved the utmost.' Current idiom says it best: 'he maxed out on life.' The evidence is overwhelming: four honorary degrees, president of three learned societies, and author of three hundred articles and thirty books. If that were not enough, in the last decade he became a fiction writer and produced a short story collection, a quartet of thrillers, and a book of poetry. Recently, Marcus launched a new religious genre with an unpublished Johannine letter in which he impersonates the fourth evangelist. His versatility was conspicuous. He wore his scholarship lightly even when his early brilliance made demands. It wasn't easy to be compared to the scholar, Mircea Eliade. It had something to do with Marcus's zest for popularization: his religious coloring books for children, classic comics on the great founders for adolescents, and dramatic religious skits for late teenagers—such pedagogy was viewed as heir to the legacies of Maria Montessori and Joseph Campbell. Yet Marcus resisted flattery. He shrugged it off as failing vision extracted its price. When Sanskrit and Arabic, Tibetan and Hebrew were too taxing to decipher, he directed his fervor toward literary ends. If in his thirties he showed the dicey side of his scholarship, in his seventies he magnified the risks. One biographer, exercising puritanical oversight, scoffed at Marcus's writing saying it resulted in a 'pedigreed mongrel.' 'It happens,' he asserted, 'in any crossbreeding of a Great Dane with a Chihuahua. The monstrous occurs when magnitude gets pressed into miniature.' Perhaps the biographer was referring to the texts for Catholic Mass requested by an ecumenical commission. No liturgist expected Marcus to draw them from six religious traditions and then place them as readings prior to the Gospel. The juxtaposition was enriching, though Marcus was accused of distorting Christian worship. He replied with his favorite expression: 'It comes with the territory.'"

Enough about his work, let me turn to the pedagogue. Some teachers project such honesty in thinking that students internalize it from conference and lecture hall. Integrity lay behind Marcus's self-effacement. You felt it as his voice lowered toward the end of a crafted sentence. He welcomed not being heard by those in the last row as they craned and strained lest any word be lost. He stressed the idea that religion is best taken as the vivid faith of persons in community; that it supports all creeds as their principle and foundation; that they derive their vivifying power from faith which is preeminent. He enjoined religionists to an overlap with the great traditions, in fact, to a virtual conversion. 'They are languages of the spirit,' he declared, 'and in our global context we are enjoined to be polyglots. You must respect their grammar and syntax even as you develop a fluency in moving from one to the other.'

"We say the style is the man. While I remember Marcus's limpid intelligence and good humor, his style lay in making it seem effortless. 'We are such wastrels with life,' he said on one occasion. 'How often we trifle on the surface. The knack of living religiously is to slip into the soul's inner sanctum without drawing attention. In that dark chamber the sanctuary lamp remains lit.' On another occasion, he counseled, 'Give back to the soil the nutrients lost in the harvest. Students are our soil. What you've learned from books, return it to them, so that they go and do likewise.' This morning we are grateful to Marcus who cultivated our lives. For as he sowed, so have we reaped."

In the reception hall Julian received warm congratulations from Marcus's colleagues:

"Julian, the psalmist got it right on the first try. In a short time you accomplished much. Thank you for revisiting Marcus's life."

"A touching tribute, Dr. Lazare. Our gratitude."

During a lull in the high praise, a young man approached him.

"Prof. Lazare, I can't thank you enough. Your words made Prof. Hoffmann live. They've prompted me to make a request. I'm Chris Meehan. Marcus Hoffmann was my thesis director. Now that he's gone, I'm at a loss for someone to direct my research. Your eulogy clinched it. I was hoping to ask you. You know him inside out."

"I'm not sure I can help, Chris. I'm not on Harvard's faculty but Columbia's."

"It would be advisory. It's only if I get stuck. I feel you could help me through scholar's block."

"Was I that assuring?"

"Yes. You made us feel Prof. Hoffmann's presence. I thought you were speaking in his person."

"You mean impersonating him?"

"Yes. No. I mean . . ."

"I understand. You couldn't say where Marcus began, and I left off. We were lost in the overlap."

"Exactly. I was wondering how that happened."

"Chalk it up to years of friendship. Something else was equally compelling. A letter."

"Really. It takes genius to imagine."

"Chris, that was Marcus's last piece of advice to me. How marvelous you know it already."

Edwards Brothers,Inc!
Thorofare, NJ 08086
13 April, 2011
BA2011103